ECONOMIC ISSUES, PROBLEMS AND PERSPECTIVES

VIRTUAL CURRENCY AND THE BITCOIN REVOLUTION

PERSPECTIVES AND CONSIDERATIONS FROM CONGRESSIONAL HEARINGS

ECONOMIC ISSUES, PROBLEMS AND PERSPECTIVES

Additional books in this series can be found on Nova's website under the Series tab.

Additional E-books in this series can be found on Nova's website under the E-book tab.

ECONOMIC ISSUES, PROBLEMS AND PERSPECTIVES

VIRTUAL CURRENCY AND THE BITCOIN REVOLUTION

PERSPECTIVES AND CONSIDERATIONS FROM CONGRESSIONAL HEARINGS

VALERIE DUSKIN
EDITOR

nova publishers
New York

For permission to use material from this book please contact us:
Telephone 631-231-7269; Fax 631-231-8175
Web Site: http://www.novapublishers.com

Additional color graphics may be available in the e-book version of this book.

Library of Congress Cataloging-in-Publication Data

ISBN: 978-1-63117-280-9

Published by Nova Science Publishers, Inc. † New York

CONTENTS

PREFACE

This book presents current information on virtual currency and the bitcoin revolution. It provides several statements and testimonies from hearings on "Beyond Silk Road: Potential Risks, Threats, and Promises of Virtual Currencies," and "The Present and Future Impact of Virtual Currency."

Chapter 1 – The Opening Statement of Thomas R. Carper, Chairman, Senate Committee on Homeland Security and Governmental Affairs.

Chapter 2 – The Statement of Jennifer Shasky Calvery, Director, Financial Crimes Enforcement Network, U.S. Department of the Treasury.

Chapter 3 – The Statement of Mythili Raman, Acting Assistant Attorney General, Criminal Division, U.S. Department of Justice.

Chapter 4 – The Testimony of Edward Lowery III, Special Agent in Charge, Criminal Investigative Division, U.S. Secret Service.

Chapter 5 – The Testimony of Patrick Murck, General Counsel, the Bitcoin Foundation.

Chapter 6 – The Testimony of Jeremy Allaire, Chairman and CEO, Circle Internet Financial.

Chapter 7 – The Testimony of Jerry Brito, Senior Research Fellow, Mercatus Center at George Mason University.

Chapter 8 – The Testimony of Ernie Allen, President and CEO, The International Centre for Missing & Exploited Children.

Chapter 9 – The Statement of Anthony Gallippi, CEO, BitPay.

Chapter 10 – The Testimony of Mercedes Kelley Tunstall, Partner and Practice Leader, Privacy and Data Security Group, Ballard Spahr LLP.

Chapter 11 – The Statement of Sarah Jane Hughes, University Scholar and Fellow in Commerical Law, Indiana University Maurer School of Law.

Chapter 12 – The Statement of Paul Smocher, BITS President, Financial Services Roundtable.

Chapter 13 – The Testimony of David J. Cotney, Commissioner of Banks, Massachusetts Division of Banks.

In: Virtual Currency …
Editor: Valerie Duskin

ISBN: 978-1-63117-280-9

Chapter 1

OPENING STATEMENT OF THOMAS R. CARPER, CHAIRMAN, SENATE COMMITTEE ON HOMELAND SECURITY AND GOVERNMENTAL AFFAIRS. HEARING ON "BEYOND SILK ROAD: POTENTIAL RISKS, THREATS, AND PROMISES OF VIRTUAL CURRENCIES"*

Over the past several months, this Committee has engaged in an investigation into the potential implications of virtual currencies. During the course of this inquiry, we've examined the issues and potential risks and threats that virtual currencies pose, as well as some of the potential promises that some believe they can bring.

In addition, we have explored with several departments and agencies throughout government how they are approaching virtual currencies as an emerging technology. This has included looking at how they are coordinating together to develop a "whole of government" approach that is consistent and informed.

Virtual currencies, perhaps most notably Bitcoin, have captured the imagination of some, struck fear among others, and confused the heck out of many of us. Indeed, based on conversations my staff and I have had with

* This is an edited, reformatted and augmented version of an opening statement, presented November 18, 2013 before the Senate Committee on Homeland Security and Governmental Affairs.

dozens of individuals both inside and outside of government, it is clear that the knowledge and expectation gaps are wide. Fundamental questions remain about what a virtual currency actually is, how it should be treated, and what the future holds.

Virtual currency can best be described as digital cash. It is generated by computers, lives on the internet, and can be used to purchase real and digital goods across the world.

Some proponents believe virtual currencies can prove valuable to those in developing countries without access to stable financial systems. Others believe it could prove to be a next generation payment system for retailers both online and in the real world.

At the same time, however, virtual currencies can be an effective tool for those looking to launder money, traffic illegal drugs, and even further the exploitation of children around the world.

While virtual currencies have seen increased attention from regulators, law enforcement, investors, and entrepreneurs in recent months, there are still many unanswered questions and unresolved issues.

This isn't the first time that advances in technology have posed challenging questions for policy makers and society as a whole. As we all know, technology is dynamic and changes quickly. Concepts like email and even the internet itself were once alien and difficult to understand and navigate. Now, most of us can read and respond to email on a device we keep in a purse or coat pocket and search the web on a multiple.

I'll be the first to admit that, like most Americans, I am no technical expert in virtual currencies. However, what I do know is that a number of smart people both inside and outside of government view this is as a major emerging issue that is deserving of our attention.

The ability to send and receive money over the internet, nearly anonymously, without a third party, has a lot of wide-ranging implications. The government needs to pay attention to this technology and to understand, and where appropriate, address these implications.

This was made all the more clear last month when federal law enforcement took down and seized an online marketplace called "the Silk Road" on which many illegal products and services were bought and sold via bitcoin. The most popular products for sale were illegal drugs and forged documents, such as ID's and passports. Other services were also for sale, including hacking services.

We're told that approximately $1.2 billion dollars in transactions were made through the Silk Road.

This site lived on what is often called the 'Dark Web,' also known as the deep web. The 'Dark Web' consists of web pages and data that are only available via special software that keeps users anonymous. Many sites and data on the "Dark Web" have been deliberately built to be untraceable in order to protect the anonymity of the user. Silk Road was one of those sites.

My understanding is that individuals could navigate to Silk Road anonymously and use Bitcoin – which can be sent to someone nearly anonymously—to make purchases.

The anonymity of the market place and near anonymity of the currency made it nearly impossible for law enforcement to track and, therefore made it an attractive place for criminal activity.

In fact, in the course of our investigation, the Department of Homeland Security informed us that the suspect who allegedly sent ricin to President Obama in April of this year was a vendor on Silk Road.

Law enforcement, including the FBI, Immigrations and Customs Enforcement, and the Secret Service should be applauded for their work in taking down a major international criminal enterprise.

But while Silk Road was perhaps the most well-known, it is not the only marketplace where illicit goods are bought and sold through bitcoin transactions. Today, a number of similar enterprises that accept bitcoins are still in business, selling weapons, child pornography, and even murder-for-hire services.

While today I suspect we will talk a lot about the well-known virtual currency Bitcoin, there are numerous other virtual currencies operating on the internet today, each with its own set of specific features.

That said, whether it is Bitcoin or any of the other virtual currencies, the federal government and society as a whole need to come together to figure out how to effectively deal with it.

Whether or not virtual currencies prove to be a boom or a bust, I think it's clear that some folks just want a chance to try and play by the rules. That's difficult to do if the rules or proper authorities aren't clear or if the future is uncertain. It's also difficult if a large number of bad apples are allowed to spoil the bunch."

In: Virtual Currency …
Editor: Valerie Duskin

ISBN: 978-1-63117-280-9

Chapter 2

STATEMENT OF JENNIFER SHASKY CALVERY, DIRECTOR, FINANCIAL CRIMES ENFORCEMENT NETWORK, U.S. DEPARTMENT OF THE TREASURY. HEARING ON "BEYOND SILK ROAD: POTENTIAL RISKS, THREATS, AND PROMISES OF VIRTUAL CURRENCIES"*

Chairman Carper, Ranking Member Coburn, and distinguished Members of the Committee, I am Jennifer Shasky Calvery, Director of the Financial Crimes Enforcement Network (FinCEN), and I appreciate the opportunity to appear before you today to discuss FinCEN's ongoing role in the Administration's efforts to establish a meaningful regulatory framework for virtual currencies that intersect with the U.S. financial system. We appreciate the Committee's interest in this important issue, and your continued support of our efforts to prevent illicit financial activity from exploiting potential gaps in our regulatory structure as technological advances create new and innovative ways to move money. I am also pleased to be testifying with my colleagues from the Departments of Justice and Homeland Security. Both play an important role in the global fight against money laundering and terrorist

* This is an edited, reformatted and augmented version of a statement, presented November 18, 2013 before the Senate Committee on Homeland Security and Governmental Affairs.

financing, and our collaboration on these issues greatly enhances the effectiveness of our efforts.

FinCEN's mission is to safeguard the financial system from illicit use, combat money laundering and promote national security through the collection, analysis, and dissemination of financial intelligence and strategic use of financial authorities. FinCEN works to achieve its mission through a broad range of interrelated strategies, including:

- Administering the Bank Secrecy Act (BSA) - the United States' primary anti-money laundering (AML)/counter-terrorist financing (CFT) regulatory regime;
- Sharing the rich financial intelligence we collect, as well as our analysis and expertise, with law enforcement, intelligence, and regulatory partners; and,
- Building global cooperation and technical expertise among financial intelligence units throughout the world.

To accomplish these activities, FinCEN employs a team comprised of approximately 340 dedicated employees with a broad range of expertise in illicit finance, financial intelligence, the financial industry, the AML/CFT regulatory regime, technology, and enforcement. We also leverage our close relationships with regulatory, law enforcement, international, and industry partners to increase our collective insight and better protect the U.S. financial system.

WHAT IS VIRTUAL CURRENCY?

Before moving into a discussion of FinCEN's role in ensuring we have smart regulation for virtual currency that is not too burdensome but also protects the U.S. financial system from illicit use, let me set the stage with some of the definitions we are using at FinCEN to understand virtual currency and the various types present in the market today.

Virtual currency is a medium of exchange that operates like a currency in some environments but does not have all the attributes of real currency. In particular, virtual currency does not have legal tender status in any jurisdiction. A *convertible* virtual currency either has an equivalent value in real currency, or acts as a substitute for real currency. In other words, it is a virtual currency that can be exchanged for real currency. At FinCEN, we have focused on two types of convertible virtual currencies: centralized and decentralized.

Centralized virtual currencies have a centralized repository and a single administrator. Liberty Reserve, which FinCEN identified earlier this year as being of primary money laundering concern pursuant to Section 311 of the USA PATRIOT Act, is an example of a centralized virtual currency. Decentralized virtual currencies, on the other hand, and as the name suggests, have no central repository and no single administrator. Instead, value is electronically transmitted between parties without an intermediary. Bitcoin is an example of a decentralized virtual currency. Bitcoin is also known as cryptocurrency, meaning that it relies on cryptographic software protocols to generate the currency and validate transactions.

There are a variety of methods an individual user might employ to obtain, spend, and then "cash out" either a centralized or decentralized virtual currency.

The following illustration shows a typical series of transactions in a centralized virtual currency, such as Liberty Reserve:

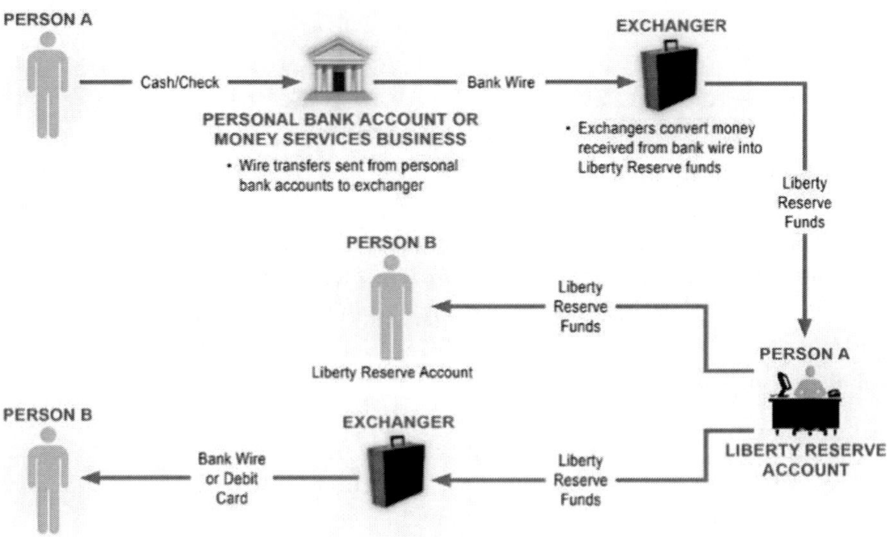

By way of comparison, the next illustration shows a very similar series of transactions in a decentralized virtual currency such as Bitcoin:

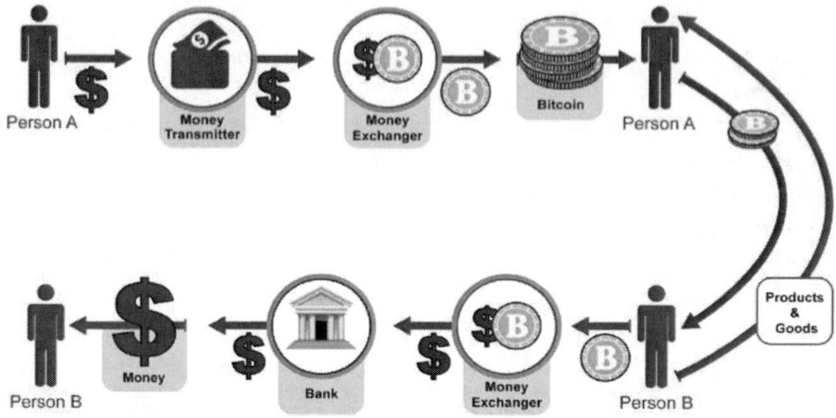

From a "follow the money" standpoint, the main difference between these two series of transactions is the absence of an "administrator" serving as intermediary in the case of Bitcoin.

This difference does have significance in FinCEN's regulatory approach to virtual currency, and that approach will be addressed further during the course of my testimony today.

Money Laundering Vulnerabilities in Virtual Currencies

Any financial institution, payment system, or medium of exchange has the potential to be exploited for money laundering or terrorist financing. Virtual currency is not different in this regard. As with all parts of the financial system, though, FinCEN seeks to understand the specific attributes that make virtual currency vulnerable to illicit use, so that we can both employ a smart regulatory approach and encourage industry to develop mitigating features in its products.

Some of the following reasons an illicit actor might decide to use a virtual currency to store and transfer value are the same reasons that legitimate users have, while other reasons are more nefarious. Specifically, an illicit actor may choose to use virtually currency because it:

- Enables the user to remain relatively anonymous;
- Is relatively simple for the user to navigate;

- May have low fees;
- Is accessible across the globe with a simple Internet connection;
- Can be used both to store value and make international transfers of value;
- Does not typically have transaction limits;
- Is generally secure;
- Features irrevocable transactions;
- Depending on the system, may have been created with the intent (and added features) to facilitate money laundering;
- If it is decentralized, has no administrator to maintain information on users and report suspicious activity to governmental authorities;
- Can exploit weaknesses in the anti-money laundering/counter terrorist financing (AML/CFT) regimes of various jurisdictions, including international disparities in, and a general lack of, regulations needed to effectively support the prevention and detection of money laundering and terrorist financing.

Because any financial institution, payment system, or medium of exchange has the potential to be exploited for money laundering, fighting such illicit use requires consistent regulation across the financial system. Virtual currency is not different from other financial products and services in this regard. What is important is that financial institutions that deal in virtual currency put effective AML/CFT controls in place to harden themselves from becoming the targets of illicit actors that would exploit any identified vulnerabilities.

Indeed, the idea that illicit actors might exploit the vulnerabilities of virtual currency to launder money is not merely theoretical. We have seen both centralized and decentralized virtual currencies exploited by illicit actors. Liberty Reserve used its centralized virtual currency as part of an alleged $6 billion money laundering operation purportedly used by criminal organizations engaged in credit card fraud, identity theft, investment fraud, computer hacking, narcotics trafficking, and child pornography. One Liberty Reserve co-founder has already pleaded guilty to money laundering in the scheme. And just recently, the Department of Justice has alleged that customers of Silk Road, the largest narcotic and contraband marketplace on the Internet to date, were required to pay in bitcoins to enable both the operator of Silk Road and its sellers to evade detection and launder hundreds of millions of dollars. With money laundering activity already valued in the billions of dollars, virtual currency is certainly worthy of FinCEN's attention.

That being said, it is also important to put virtual currency in perspective as a payment system. The U.S. government indictment and proposed special measures against Liberty Reserve allege it was involved in laundering more than $6 billion. Administrators of other major centralized virtual currencies report processing similar transaction volumes to what Liberty Reserve did. In the case of Bitcoin, it has been publicly reported that its users processed transactions worth approximately $8 billion over the twelve-month period preceding October 2013; however, this measure may be artificially high due to the extensive use of automated layering in many Bitcoin transactions. By way of comparison, according to information reported publicly, in 2012 Bank of America processed $244.4 trillion in wire transfers, PayPal processed approximately $145 billion in online payments, Western Union made remittances totaling approximately $81 billion, the Automated Clearing House (ACH) Network processed more than 21 billion transactions with a total dollar value of $36.9 trillion, and Fedwire, which handles large-scale wholesale transfers, processed 132 million transactions for a total of $599 trillion. This relative volume of transactions becomes important when you consider that, according to the United Nations Office on Drugs and Crime (UNODC), the best estimate for the amount of all global criminal proceeds available for laundering through the financial system in 2009 was $1.6 trillion. While of growing concern, to date, virtual currencies have yet to overtake more traditional methods to move funds internationally, whether for legitimate or criminal purposes.

Mitigating Money Laundering Vulnerabilities in Virtual Currencies

FinCEN's main goal in administering the BSA is to ensure the integrity and transparency of the U.S. financial system so that money laundering and terrorist financing can be prevented and, where it does occur, be detected for follow on action. One of our biggest challenges is striking the right balance between the costs and benefits of regulation. One strategy we use to address this challenge is to promote consistency, where possible, in our regulatory framework across different parts of the financial services industry. It ensures a level playing field for industry and minimizes gaps in our AML/CFT coverage.

Recognizing the emergence of new payment methods and the potential for abuse by illicit actors, FinCEN began working with our law enforcement and regulatory partners several years ago to study the issue. We understood that AML protections must keep pace with the emergence of new payment systems, such as virtual currency and prepaid cards, lest those innovations become a favored tool of illicit actors. In July 2011, after a public comment period designed to receive feedback from industry, FinCEN released two rules that update several definitions and provide the needed flexibility to accommodate innovation in the payment systems space under our preexisting regulatory framework. Those rules are: (1) Definitions and Other Regulations Relating to Money Services Businesses; and (2) Definitions and Other Regulations Relating to Prepaid Access.

The updated definitions reflect FinCEN's earlier guidance and rulings, as well as current business operations in the industry. As such, they have been able to accommodate the development of new payment systems, including virtual currency. Specifically, the new rule on money services businesses added the phrase "other value that substitutes for currency" to the definition of "money transmission services." And since a convertible virtual currency either has an equivalent value in real currency, or acts a substitute for real currency, it qualifies as "other value that substitutes for currency" under the definition of "money transmission services." A person that provides money transmission services is a "money transmitter," a type of money services business already covered by the AML/CFT protections in the BSA.

As a follow-up to the regulations and in an effort to provide additional clarity on the compliance expectations for those actors involved in virtual currency transactions subject to FinCEN oversight, on March 18, 2013, FinCEN supplemented its money services business regulations with interpretive guidance designed to clarify the applicability of the regulations implementing the BSA to persons creating, obtaining, distributing, exchanging, accepting, or transmitting virtual currencies. In the simplest of terms, FinCEN's guidance explains that administrators or exchangers of virtual currencies must register with FinCEN, and institute certain recordkeeping, reporting and AML program control measures, unless an exception to these requirements applies. The guidance also explains that those who use virtual currencies exclusively for common personal transactions like buying goods or services online are users, not subject to regulatory requirements under the BSA. In all cases, FinCEN employs an activity-based test to determine when someone dealing with virtual currency qualifies as a money transmitter. The guidance clarifies definitions and expectations to ensure that businesses engaged in such activities are aware of their regulatory responsibilities, including registering appropriately. Furthermore, FinCEN closely coordinates with its state regulatory counterparts to encourage appropriate application of FinCEN guidance as part of the states' separate AML compliance oversight of financial institutions.

It is in the best interest of virtual currency providers to comply with these regulations for a number of reasons. First is the idea of corporate responsibility. Legitimate financial institutions, including virtual currency providers, do not go into business with the aim of laundering money on behalf of criminals. Virtual currencies are a financial service, and virtual currency administrators and exchangers are financial institutions. As I stated earlier, any financial institution could be exploited for money laundering purposes. What is important is for institutions to put controls in place to deal with those money laundering threats, and to meet their AML reporting obligations.

At the same time, being a good corporate citizen and complying with regulatory responsibilities is good for a company's bottom line. Every financial institution needs to be concerned about its reputation and show that it is operating with transparency and integrity within the bounds of the law. Legitimate customers will be drawn to a virtual currency or administrator or exchanger where they know their money is safe and where they know the company has a reputation for integrity. And banks will want to provide services to administrators or exchangers that show not only great innovation, but also great integrity and transparency.

The decision to bring virtual currency within the scope of our regulatory framework should be viewed by those who respect and obey the basic rule of law as a positive development for this sector. It recognizes the innovation virtual currencies provide, and the benefits they might offer society. Several new payment methods in the financial sector have proven their capacity to empower customers, encourage the development of innovative financial products, and expand access to financial services. We want these advances to continue. However, those institutions that choose to act outside of their AML obligations and outside of the law have and will continue to be held accountable. FinCEN will do everything in its regulatory power to stop such abuses of the U.S. financial system.

As previously mentioned, earlier this year, FinCEN identified Liberty Reserve as a financial institution of primary money laundering concern under Section 311 of the USA PATRIOT Act. Liberty Reserve operated as an online, virtual currency, money transfer system conceived and operated specifically to allow – and encourage – illicit use because of the anonymity it offered. It was deliberately designed to avoid regulatory scrutiny and tailored its services to illicit actors looking to launder their ill-gotten gains. According to the allegations contained in a related criminal action brought by the U.S. Department of Justice, those illicit actors included criminal organizations engaged in credit card fraud, identity theft, investment fraud, computer hacking, narcotics trafficking, and child pornography, just to name a few. The 311 action taken by FinCEN was designed to restrict the ability of Liberty Reserve to access the U.S. financial system, publicly notify the international financial community of the risks posed by Liberty Reserve, and to send a resounding message to other offshore money launderers that such abuse of the U.S. financial system will not be tolerated and their activity can be reached through our targeted financial measures.

Sharing Our Knowledge and Expertise on Virtual Currency

As the financial intelligence unit for the United States, FinCEN must stay current on how money is being laundered in the United States, including through new and emerging payment systems, so that we can share this expertise with our many law enforcement, regulatory, industry, and foreign financial intelligence unit partners, and effectively serve as the cornerstone of this country's AML/CFT regime. FinCEN has certainly sought to meet this responsibility with regard to virtual currency and its exploitation by illicit actors. In doing so, we have drawn and continue to draw from the knowledge we have gained through our regulatory efforts, use of targeted financial measures, analysis of the financial intelligence we collect, independent study of virtual currency, outreach to industry, and collaboration with our many partners in law enforcement.

In the same month we issued our guidance on virtual currency, March 2013, FinCEN also issued a Networking Bulletin on crypto-currencies to provide a more granular explanation of this highly complex industry to law enforcement and assist it in following the money as it funnels between virtual currency channels and the U.S. financial system. Among other things, the bulletin addresses the role of traditional banks, money transmitters, and exchangers that come into play as intermediaries by enabling users to fund the purchase of virtual currencies and exchange virtual currencies for other types of currency. It also highlights known records processes associated with virtual currencies and the potential value these records may offer to investigative officials. The bulletin has been in high demand since its publication and the feedback regarding its tremendous value has come from the entire spectrum of our law enforcement partners. In fact, demand for more detailed information on crypto-currencies has been so high that we have also shared it with several of our regulatory and foreign financial intelligence unit partners.

One feature of a FinCEN Networking Bulletin is that it asks the readers to provide ongoing feedback on what they are learning through their investigations so that we can create a forum to quickly learn of new developments, something particularly important with a new payment method. Based on what we are learning through this forum and other means, FinCEN has issued several analytical products of a tactical nature to inform law enforcement operations.

Equally important to our ongoing efforts to deliver expertise to our law enforcement partners is FinCEN's engagement with our regulatory counterparts to ensure they are kept apprised of the latest trends in virtual currencies and the potential vulnerabilities they pose to traditional financial institutions under their supervision. FinCEN uses its collaboration with the Federal Financial Institutions Examination Council (FFIEC) BSA Working Group as a platform to review and discuss FinCEN's regulations and guidance, and the most recent and relevant trends in virtual currencies. One such example occurred just recently, when several FinCEN virtual currency experts gave a comprehensive presentation on the topic to an audience of Federal and state bank examiners at an FFIEC Payment Systems Risk Conference. The presentation covered an overview of virtual currency operations, FinCEN's guidance on the application of FinCEN regulations to virtual currency, enforcement actions, and ongoing industry outreach efforts.

FinCEN also participates in the FBI-led Virtual Currency Emerging Threats Working Group, the FDIC-led Cyber Fraud Working Group, the Terrorist Financing & Financial Crimes-led Treasury Cyber Working Group, and with a community of other financial intelligence units. We host speakers, discuss current trends, and provide information on FinCEN resources and authorities as we work with our partners in an effort to foster an open line of communication across the government regarding bad actors involved in virtual currency and cyber-related crime.

Finally, FinCEN has shared its strategic analysis on money laundering through virtual currency with executives at many of our partner law enforcement and regulatory agencies, and foreign financial intelligence units, as well as with U.S. government policy makers.

Outreach to the Virtual Currency Industry

Recognizing that the new, expanded definition of money transmission would bring new financial entities under the purview of FinCEN's regulatory framework, shortly after the publication of the interpretive guidance and as part of FinCEN's ongoing commitment to engage in dialogue with the financial industry and continually learn more about the industries that we regulate, FinCEN announced its interest in holding outreach meetings with representatives from the virtual currency industry. The meetings are designed to hear feedback on the implications of recent regulatory responsibilities imposed on this industry, and to receive industry's input on where additional guidance would be helpful to facilitate compliance.

We held the first such meeting with representatives of the Bitcoin Foundation on August 26, 2013 at FinCEN's Washington, DC offices and included attendees from a cross-section of the law enforcement and regulatory communities. This outreach was part of FinCEN's overall efforts to increase knowledge and understanding of the regulated industry and how its members are impacted by regulations, and thereby help FinCEN most efficiently and effectively work with regulated entities to further the common goals of the detection and deterrence of financial crime. To further capitalize on this important dialogue and exchange of ideas, FinCEN has invited the Bitcoin Foundation to provide a similar presentation at the next plenary of the Bank Secrecy Act Advisory Group (BSAAG) scheduled for mid-December. The BSAAG is a Congressionally-chartered forum that brings together representatives from the financial industry, law enforcement, and the regulatory community to advise FinCEN on the functioning of our AML/CFT regime.

Conclusion

The Administration has made appropriate oversight of the virtual currency industry a priority, and as a result, FinCEN's efforts in this regard have increased significantly over recent years through targeted regulatory measures, outreach to regulatory and law enforcement counterparts and our partners in the private sector, and the development of expertise. We are very encouraged by the progress we have made thus far. We are dedicated to continuing to build on these accomplishments by remaining focused on future trends in the virtual currency industry and how they may inform potential changes to our regulatory framework for the future. Thank you for inviting me to testify before you today. I would be happy to answer any questions you may have.

In: Virtual Currency …
Editor: Valerie Duskin
ISBN: 978-1-63117-280-9

Chapter 3

STATEMENT OF MYTHILI RAMAN, ACTING ASSISTANT ATTORNEY GENERAL, CRIMINAL DIVISION, U.S. DEPARTMENT OF JUSTICE. HEARING ON "BEYOND SILK ROAD: POTENTIAL RISKS, THREATS, AND PROMISES OF VIRTUAL CURRENCIES"*

Chairman Carper, Ranking Member Coburn, and distinguished Members of the Committee: Thank you for the opportunity to appear before the Committee today to discuss the Department of Justice's work regarding virtual currencies. I am honored to represent the Department at this hearing and to describe for you our approach to virtual currencies, our recent successes in prosecuting criminals who use virtual currencies for illicit purposes, and some of the challenges we face as virtual currency systems continue to evolve.

INTRODUCTION

The Department of Justice recognizes that many virtual currency systems offer legitimate financial services and have the potential to promote more efficient global commerce. We have also seen, however, that certain aspects of

* This is an edited, reformatted and augmented version of a statement, presented November 18, 2013 before the Senate Committee on Homeland Security and Governmental Affairs.

virtual currencies appeal to criminals and present a host of new challenges to law enforcement.

The concept of virtual currencies is not new to the Department and, indeed, the Department has investigated and prosecuted the illicit use of virtual currencies since the late 1990s, when criminals first began using systems such as WebMoney and e-Gold to conduct their business. Over the last 15 years, however, virtual currencies have evolved and diversified significantly, challenging the Department to adapt our capabilities to deal with new systems and threats.

As with all emerging technologies, the Department has aggressively used our existing tools and capabilities to combat illegal activities involving virtual currencies. The Department has two primary law enforcement interests in virtual currency: (1) deterring and prosecuting criminals using virtual currency systems to move or hide money that is used to facilitate, or is derived from, criminal or terrorist acts, *i.e.*, money laundering; and (2) investigating and prosecuting those virtual currency services that themselves violate laws aimed at illegal money transmission and money laundering. As I will describe in my testimony, the Department is committed to using all the tools at our disposal to ensure that those law enforcement interests are met, even as virtual currency systems evolve.

ILLICIT USE

"Virtual currency" is a medium of exchange circulated over a network, typically the Internet, which is not backed by a government. These systems can be both centralized and decentralized.

Early centralized models, where the currency is controlled by a single private entity, have expanded and now encompass a wide range of business concepts. Some centralized virtual currencies take the form of digital precious metals, such as e-Gold and Pecunix, where users exchange digital currency units ostensibly backed by gold bullion or other precious metals. Others exist within popular online games or virtual worlds, such as Farmville, Second Life, or World of Warcraft. Still others are online payment systems such as WebMoney and Liberty Reserve, which are available generally outside of specific online communities and denominate users' accounts in virtual currency rather than U.S. Dollars, Euros, or some other national currency. Decentralized systems such as Bitcoin, which have no centralized administrating authority and instead operate as peer-to-peer transaction networks, entered the scene relatively recently but are growing rapidly. A network of sites and services, including exchangers who buy and sell virtual currencies in exchange for national currencies or other mediums of value, have developed around virtual currency systems, as well.

Criminals are nearly always early adopters of new technologies and financial systems, and virtual currency is no exception. As virtual currency has grown, it has attracted illicit users along with legitimate ones. Our experience has shown that some criminals have exploited virtual currency systems because of the ability of those systems to conduct transfers quickly, securely, and often with a perceived higher level of anonymity than that afforded by traditional financial services. The irreversibility of many virtual currency transactions additionally appeals to a variety of individuals seeking to engage in illicit activity, as does their ability to send funds cross-border.

Cyber criminals were among the first illicit groups to take widespread advantage of virtual currency. We have seen that many players in the cyber underground rely on virtual currency to conduct financial transactions. Early users of virtual currency also included criminals involved in the trafficking of child pornography, credit card fraud, identity theft, and high-yield investment schemes. As virtual currency became more widespread and criminals became increasingly computer savvy, other criminal groups moved to capitalize on virtual currency, as well. There are now public examples of virtual currency being used by nearly every type of criminal imaginable.

It is not surprising that criminals are drawn to services that allow users to conduct financial transactions while remaining largely anonymous. And, indeed, some of the criminal activity occurs through online black markets, many of which operate as Tor hidden services. Tor hidden services are sites accessible only through Tor, an anonymizing network that masks users' Internet traffic by routing it through a series of volunteer servers, called "nodes," across the globe. Online black markets capitalize on Tor's anonymizing features to offer a wide selection of illicit goods and services, ranging from pornographic images of children to dangerous narcotics to stolen credit card information.

At the same time, we have seen that though virtual currency systems are growing rapidly, few systems currently exist that could easily accommodate the hundreds of millions of dollars often moved in a single large-scale money laundering scheme. Transaction size is limited by the carrying capacity of the virtual currency systems and the exchangers. When taken in the aggregate, however, the relatively small dollar values associated with most illicit virtual currency transactions quickly add up. At their prime, e-Gold and Liberty

Reserve, two virtual currency systems prosecuted by the Department, each moved the equivalent of over $1 billion in illegal proceeds annually. As virtual currencies grow, the capacity for larger single transactions grows, as well.

The Department has prosecuted several of these systems, such as e-Gold, based on evidence that they can be, and often are, intentionally designed to facilitate illegal activity. These services typically do not conduct any meaningful customer due diligence and do not screen for transactions related to money laundering or terrorist financing. At the same time, these complicit and illicit businesses allow users to conceal their identities and maintain high levels of anonymity during transactions.

To be clear, virtual currency is not necessarily synonymous with anonymity. A convertible virtual currency with appropriate anti-money laundering and know-your-customer controls, as required by U.S. law, can safeguard its system from exploitation by criminals and terrorists in the same way any other money services business could. As virtual currency systems develop, it is imperative to law enforcement interests that those systems comply with applicable anti-money laundering and know-your-customer controls.

DEPARTMENT ACTIONS

Exploitation by malicious actors is a problem faced by all types of financial services and is not unique to virtual currency systems. Although malicious actors have utilized emerging technologies to further their criminal schemes, the Department has thus far been able to apply existing tools to ensure vigorous prosecution of these schemes.

The Department relies on money services business, money transmission, and anti-money laundering statutes to curtail this sort of unlawful activity. Many virtual currency systems, exchangers, and related services operate as money transmitters, which are part of a larger class of institutions called money services businesses. Money transmitters are required under 31 U.S.C. § 5330 to register with the Financial Crimes Enforcement Network (FinCEN). Most states also require money transmitters to obtain a state license in order to conduct business in the state. Any money transmitter that fails to register with FinCEN or to obtain the requisite state licensing may be subject to criminal prosecution under 18 U.S.C. § 1960. Additionally, the general money laundering and spending statutes, 18 U.S.C. §§ 1956 and 1957, cover financial transactions involving virtual currencies. Finally, where virtual currencies are used in furtherance of underlying criminal activity, the Department can rely on traditional criminal statutes proscribing that activity, such as narcotics, cybercrime, child exploitation, and firearms laws.

Some of the major prosecutions in recent years involving virtual currency services are as follows.

E-Gold

The Department first took major action against an illicit virtual currency service in 2007, when it indicted e-Gold and its three principal owners on charges related to money laundering and operating an unlicensed money transmitting business. E-Gold offered digital accounts purportedly backed by physical gold bullion. A valid e-mail address was the only information required to set up an account, allowing users to conduct highly anonymous international transactions over the Internet. As a result, e-Gold became a popular payment method for sellers of child pornography, operators of investment scams, and perpetrators of credit card and identity fraud. At its peak, e-Gold reportedly moved over $6 million each day for more than 2.5 million accounts. In 2008, e-Gold and the three individuals pleaded guilty.

Liberty Reserve

Following the e-Gold indictment, several similar but smaller systems and exchangers were indicted or closed themselves down to evade law enforcement detection. According to publicly filed charging documents, an executive of one of those businesses, Arthur Budovsky, then set out to create Liberty Reserve, an improved centralized virtual currency variation allegedly designed to evade U.S. law enforcement. Among other things, Liberty Reserve operated offshore – it was based in Costa Rica – and purportedly recommended that its customers use money exchangers located in countries without significant governmental money-laundering oversight or regulation. Moreover, Budovsky, the principal founder of Liberty Reserve, was so committed to avoiding the reach of U.S. law that, according to the indictment, in 2011, he formally renounced his U.S. citizenship and became a Costa Rican citizen in order to avoid facing justice in the United States.

Despite Budovsky's alleged efforts, earlier this year, the Department indicted Liberty Reserve and its executives, including Budovsky, for running a

$6 billion money laundering operation. In a coordinated action, the Department of the Treasury identified Liberty Reserve as a financial institution of primary money laundering concern under Section 311 of the USA PATRIOT Act, effectively cutting it off from the U.S. financial system.

According to the indictment, Liberty Reserve allowed users to send and receive funds with a high level of anonymity by not requiring users to validate their identities and allowing users to make untraceable fund transfers in exchange for a privacy fee. Many of the transactions were sent to or from users in the United States, but Liberty Reserve never registered with the appropriate U.S. authorities. As revealed in the Department's filings, Liberty Reserve became a system of choice for cyber criminals and was used in a wide array of illegal activity, including credit card fraud, identity theft, investment fraud, computer hacking, and child pornography. As a result of the Department's action, the site was shuttered and effectively put out of business, and seven defendants were charged. One is in custody in the United States, one has entered a guilty plea, three others, including the lead defendant Budovsky, are pending extradition, and two others are at large. The case exemplifies the Department's resolve to pursue purported major money laundering facilitators, even those who hide offshore.

Silk Road

Just last month, the Department took action against one of the most popular online black markets, Silk Road. Allegedly operated by a U.S. citizen living in California at the time of his arrest, Silk Road accepted bitcoins exclusively as a payment mechanism on its site. The Department's complaint alleges that, in less than three years, Silk Road served as a venue for over 100,000 buyers to purchase hundreds of kilograms of illegal drugs and other illicit goods from several thousand drug dealers and other criminal vendors. The site also purportedly laundered the proceeds of these transactions, amounting to hundreds of millions of dollars in bitcoins. In addition to arresting the site's operator and shutting down the service, the Department to date has seized over 170 thousand bitcoins, valued as of this past Friday, November 15, 2013, at over $70 million.

A separate indictment charges Silk Road's operator with drug distribution conspiracy, attempted witness murder, and using interstate commerce facilities in the commission of murderfor-hire. With regard to the murder-related charges, the indictment alleges that the Silk Road operator paid an undercover federal agent to murder one of the operator's employees.

UNIQUE CHALLENGES

The cases I just described illustrate not only Department successes in combating illicit use of virtual currency, but also many of the challenges investigators face when they encounter these systems, some of which may ultimately require additional legal or regulatory tools.

Virtual currency allows users to send money across the globe without dealing with a traditional financial institution. While this feature provides several benefits for legitimate customers, it can significantly complicate law enforcement efforts to follow the money.

Virtual currency systems have a global reach and clientele. Virtual currency businesses can cater to U.S. clientele while operating on the other side of the world. Investigations into illicit virtual currency businesses therefore often require considerable cooperation from international partners. The Liberty Reserve investigation and takedown, for example, involved coordinated law enforcement action in 17 countries.

The international nature of the transactions poses an additional challenge where the overseas regulatory regime treats virtual currency differently or, as is true in some cases, fails to cover it at all. While this challenge may diminish with the Financial Action Task Force's recent guidance addressing the need for all countries to develop a risk-based approach to new payment products and services, incongruent regulatory regimes will likely remain a challenge when dealing with virtual currency services overseas.

Among the most significant challenges the Department faces in dealing with virtual currency is the difficulty in obtaining customer records. Because decentralized systems lack any sort of administering authority to collect user information or receive legal process, investigators must rely on information collected by other sources, such as exchangers. Even if the target used a centralized system or exchanger, however, accurate customer records may still be difficult to obtain, or may not exist at all. Illicit users are typically attracted to systems with lax anti-money laundering and know-your-customer controls. These services often attempt to evade U.S. action by operating out of countries that have poor regulatory oversight and are less willing to cooperate with U.S. law enforcement. Even if the system at issue operates in a country with effective regulation and a cooperative relationship with the United States, the legal process for obtaining foreign records is relatively slow when compared to the near-instantaneous speed at which the virtual currency user can send the funds to another jurisdiction.

A final challenge arises from the link between virtual currency and encryption. Decentralized virtual currencies typically rely on an encryption algorithm, rather than a central authority, to administer the currency. These encryption-based currencies, also known as cryptocurrencies, lack a central administering authority that might otherwise possess valuable evidence. In addition, users of these currencies often encrypt their digital wallets, complicating our efforts to seize and forfeit criminal proceeds.

COLLABORATIVE EFFORTS

The Department recognizes that virtual currency's ability to facilitate the global movement of funds by a wide array of illicit actors necessitates a comprehensive and collaborative approach with our domestic and international partners. To promote such coordination, the Department is an active participant in the Virtual Currency Emerging Threats Working Group (VCET). VCET was founded by the Federal Bureau of Investigation (FBI) in early 2012 to mitigate the cross-programmatic threats arising from illicit actors' use of virtual currency systems. The group leverages the collective subject matter expertise of its members to address issues arising from illicit actors' use of virtual currency, and deconflicts and shares information and concerns. VCET members represent an array of U.S. Government agencies, including, within the Department, the FBI, the Drug Enforcement Administration, multiple U.S. Attorney's Offices, and the Criminal Division's Asset Forfeiture and Money Laundering Section and Computer Crime and Intellectual Property Section.

The Department contributes to several additional interagency groups concerning virtual currencies and emerging payment systems, including the New Payment Methods Ad Hoc Working Group, a subgroup of the Terrorist Finance Working Group, led by the State Department. The FBI specifically has issued numerous intelligence products related to virtual currency, many of which were coauthored with other members of the U.S. Intelligence Community.

The Department is committed to working with our regulatory partners to ensure appropriate coordination on regulatory issues related to virtual currency. The Department participated in meetings and discussions with FinCEN regarding the July 2011 Final Rule on Money Services Businesses and its applicability to virtual currencies, as well as the related March 18, 2013, FinCEN guidance. The Department regards FinCEN's regulation of many virtual currency services as money transmitters, as well as the resulting applicability of anti-money laundering and know-your-customer requirements under the Bank Secrecy Act, as crucial tools in preventing malicious actors from exploiting virtual currency systems in furtherance of illicit activity.

The Department works closely with FinCEN and the Department of Treasury to coordinate enforcement actions when appropriate. This relationship allowed the Department to unseal the Liberty Reserve indictment in coordination with Treasury's announcement naming the company as a financial institution of primary money laundering concern under Section 311 of the USA PATRIOT Act. Such coordinated actions are integral tools in combating illicit finance.

FUTURE TRENDS

The Department anticipates that virtual currency will continue to evolve and grow in popularity. That growth inevitably will be accompanied by an increase in illicit transactions, which makes it critical that virtual currency services understand their legal obligations and requirements. The Department is encouraged by the increasing prominence of legitimate virtual currency services that are attempting to comply with U.S. law. While a number of services have registered at the federal level, many are still struggling with implementing appropriate anti-money laundering, know-your-customer, and customer due diligence programs, as well as complying with state-level regulations and licensing requirements. As members of the U.S. financial community, virtual currency services can and must safeguard themselves from exploitation by criminals and terrorists by implementing legally required anti-money laundering and know-your-customer controls.

As the Administration's Strategy to Combat Transnational Organized Crime recognizes, transnational organized crime networks are increasingly involved in cybercrime, and can imperil consumers' faith in emerging digital systems. We must also pay close attention to the critical role of facilitators who cross both the licit and illicit worlds and provide services to legitimate customers and criminals alike.

The Department recognizes that malicious actors are often resourceful, and even legitimate virtual currency services can become unwitting conduits for illicit transactions when these actors are able to defeat or circumvent anti-money laundering controls. Outreach to these systems, much as the Department conducts with the formal financial sector, is an important tool in combating the exploitation of the systems for criminal and terrorist purposes. Because centralized payment systems and exchangers often interact with the traditional financial sector and hold bank accounts at major financial institutions, the range of such Department outreach extends to the financial services community at large, complementing the outreach and training efforts of FinCEN, the primary BSA regulator, and the Department of the Treasury. Department of Justice personnel routinely provide trainings to the private sector, as well as to domestic and international law enforcement and intelligence personnel, and specifically address virtual currency.

Law enforcement, Congress, and regulators must remain vigilant to ensure that the U.S. legal and regulatory structure is sufficiently robust to cover decentralized virtual currencies. The Department looks forward to working with Congress to ensure that law enforcement continues to have the tools necessary to combat the use of virtual currency for illicit purposes.

CONCLUSION

Chairman Carper and Ranking Member Coburn, I thank you for this opportunity to discuss the Department's work on virtual currency.

I look forward to any questions that you may have.

In: Virtual Currency …
Editor: Valerie Duskin
ISBN: 978-1-63117-280-9

Chapter 4

TESTIMONY OF EDWARD LOWERY III, SPECIAL AGENT IN CHARGE, CRIMINAL INVESTIGATIVE DIVISION, U.S. SECRET SERVICE. HEARING ON "BEYOND SILK ROAD: POTENTIAL RISKS, THREATS, AND PROMISES OF VIRTUAL CURRENCIES"*

Good afternoon Chairman Carper, Ranking Member Coburn, and distinguished Members of the Committee. Thank you for the opportunity to testify on behalf of the U.S. Department of Homeland Security (DHS) regarding the risks and challenges posed by digital currencies[1] and the role of the U.S. Secret Service (Secret Service) in investigating crimes associated with online payment systems. Fraudulent schemes and money laundering are the Secret Service's chief concerns with respect to digital currencies and the facilitation of other serious crimes. The Secret Service is committed to adapting to evolving cyber threats by conducting robust investigations of offenses involving digital currencies within its jurisdiction in order to effectively suppress criminal activity.

As the original guardian of the nation's financial payment systems, since 1865 the Secret Service has conducted investigations to protect American consumers, industries, financial institutions, and critical infrastructure from criminal exploit. Accordingly, the Secret Service has extensive authority and

---

* This is an edited, reformatted and augmented version of a testimony, presented November 18, 2013 before the Senate Committee on Homeland Security and Governmental Affairs.

responsibility to investigate financial crimes and dismantle the infrastructure that supports these criminal activities, including when these crimes are conducted through cyberspace. In executing our mission, the Secret Service closely partners with Federal, state, local, and international law enforcement agencies and other interagency partners. Notably, the Secret Service and U.S. Immigration and Customs Enforcement's Homeland Security Investigations (ICE/HSI)[2] partner through the Secret Service's Electronic Crimes Task Forces (ECTFs),[3] which leverage the private sector, academia, and state and local law enforcement to support cyber crime investigations. As former Department of Treasury law enforcement agencies, the Secret Service and ICE/HSI partner closely with the Financial Crimes Enforcement Network (FinCEN) and the Department of Treasury in conducting financial crime investigations. In addition, the Secret Service and ICE/HSI participate in the Virtual Currency Threats Working Group and other collaborative efforts with regulators and the national security staff to address the challenges posed by digital currencies and new payment systems.

Over the past decade, in addition to their many legitimate uses, digital currencies—by which I mean digital representations of both real national currencies, or fiat currency, and virtual currencies, which do not constitute the legal tender of any jurisdiction—have attracted malicious actors seeking to hide illicit money transactions. Accordingly, the Secret Service has developed extensive experience in conducting investigations that involve digital currencies. The Secret Service and its interagency partners have investigated and shutdown two major illicit providers of digital currencies that supported extensive criminal activity: e-Gold Ltd. in 2007 and Liberty Reserve earlier this year. Additionally, the Secret Service investigated and shutdown illicit digital currency exchangers, such as Western Express. This successful investigation and prosecution recently concluded with 15 convictions, thanks to the dedicated eight-year effort of the Manhattan District Attorney's Office and the Secret Service's New York/New Jersey ECTF. These and other criminal investigations have provided the Secret Service with a better understanding of the risks and challenges posed by digital currencies.

Criminal Use of Digital Currencies

In recent years, digital currencies have become a preferred form of money for criminals to conduct their illicit activities. Digital currencies provide an efficient means of moving large sums of money globally for both legitimate and criminal purposes. However, as a form of virtual currency,[4] many digital currencies attempt to operate outside the legal and regulatory systems many countries have established to govern legal tender. Additionally, digital currencies often provide a greater anonymity than the traditional banking system. These attributes make digital currencies a preferred tool of transnational criminal organizations for conducting their criminal activities, transmitting their illicit revenue internationally, and laundering their profits.

Based on Secret Service investigations into the criminal use of digital currencies, criminals prefer those they assess to offer:

1. The greatest degree of anonymity for both users and transactions.
2. The ability to quickly and confidently move illicit proceeds from one country to another.
3. Low volatility, which results in lower exchange risk, increasing the digital currency's ability to be an efficient means to transmit and store wealth.
4. Widespread adoption in the criminal underground.
5. Trustworthiness.

Consequently, as part of its mission to suppress criminal activity, the Secret Service's investigations into digital currency exchangers and administrators have focused on those currencies with the above attributes that play an instrumental role in enabling large-scale criminal activity in violation of laws under Secret Service jurisdiction.[5]

Digital currencies differ as to their principal criminal uses. Some digital currencies are primarily used to purchase illicit goods and services (e.g., drugs, credit card information, personally identifiable information (PII), and other contraband or criminal services). Other digital currencies are primarily used for money laundering: concealing transactions involving large amounts of money—particularly transnational transfers. The greatest risks are posed by digital currencies that have widespread use for both of these criminal purposes: e-Gold and Liberty Reserve are prime examples of these high-risk digital currencies.

e-Gold

e-Gold was founded in 1996 and offered a pseudonymous digital currency that was originally backed with gold coins stored in a safe deposit box in

Florida. A valid email address was the only information that was required to open an e-Gold account. Although other contact information was requested, it was not verified. Thousands of e-Gold users opened their accounts with blatantly false information, such as using the names "Mickey Mouse" or "Donald Duck," among others. Once people opened e-Gold accounts, they could fund them by using exchangers who converted U.S. currency into e-Gold. When these accounts were established and funded, the account holders could gain access through the Internet and conduct anonymous transactions with other e-Gold account holders anywhere in the world.

e-Gold quickly became the preferred financial transaction method of transnational cyber criminals—particularly those involved in the trafficking of stolen financial information and PII of U.S. citizens—and a tool for money laundering by cyber criminals. Criminals' reliance on e-Gold to facilitate certain crimes, including the purchase of child pornography and money laundering, made it the focus of a successful joint investigation by the Secret Service, IRS Criminal Investigations (IRS-CI), the Federal Bureau of Investigation, and the Florida-based St. Cloud Internal Revenue Service-Secret Service Financial Crimes and Money Laundering Task Force. The case was prosecuted by the U.S. Attorney's Office for the District of Columbia, the Department of Justice's Computer Crime and Intellectual Property Section and Asset Forfeiture and Money Laundering Section (AFMLS), with assistance from the Criminal Division's Child Exploitation and Obscenity Section. e-Gold and its corporate affiliate pled guilty to money laundering and operating an unlicensed money transmitting business. The principal director of e-Gold and its corporate affiliate, as well as senior leaders, pled guilty to conspiracy to engage in money laundering and operating an unlicensed money transmitting business. e-Gold's gold reserve was liquidated for $90 million to allow legitimate account holders to claim their assets. As of December 18, 2012, over $10.8 million contained in 12,869 accounts has been forfeited to the Federal Government as part of an on-going asset forfeiture process.

Liberty Reserve[6]

Liberty Reserve was a Costa Rica-based digital currency service that provided what it described as "instant, real-time currency for international commerce" that can be used to "send and receive payments from anyone, anywhere on the globe." Additionally, Liberty Reserve described itself as the Internet's "largest payment processor and money transfer system," serving "millions" of people around the world, including the United States. The alleged principal founder of Liberty Reserve moved to Costa Rica to operate Liberty Reserve after being convicted in the United States in December 2006 for operating "Gold Age, Inc." as an unlicensed money transmitting business.

Liberty Reserve was allegedly designed to make anonymous and untraceable financial transactions to support criminal activity and elude law enforcement. Liberty Reserve quickly became the predominant digital currency used for money laundering by transnational organized cyber crime and other criminals. Before the Secret Service-led investigation shutdown Liberty Reserve, it was estimated to have had more than one million users worldwide, with more than 200,000 users in the United States, and to have processed more than 12 million financial transactions, with a combined value of more than $1.4 billion annually. Overall, from 2006 to May of 2013, Liberty Reserve allegedly processed at least 55 million separate financial transactions and is believed to have laundered more than $6 billion in criminal proceeds.[7]

On May 24, 2013, five individuals were arrested in Costa Rica, Spain, and New York for operating Liberty Reserve under charges for conspiracy to commit money laundering and conspiracy and operation of an unlicensed money transmitting business. At the same time, in close coordination with this law enforcement action, the Department of the Treasury identified Liberty Reserve as a financial institution of primary money laundering concern under Section 311 of the USA PATRIOT Act, effectively cutting it off from the U.S. financial system.

Liberty Reserve's alleged role in supporting criminal activity made its shut down a high priority of numerous law enforcement agencies. The Secret Service worked closely with IRS-CI and ICE/HSI as part of the Global Illicit Financial Team (GIFT) to conduct this investigation, and the Secret Service New York/New Jersey ECTF provided vital assistance. In addition, the cooperation and assistance of international law enforcement partners, including the Judicial Investigation Organization in Costa Rica, the National High Tech Crime Unit in the Netherlands, the Spanish National Police, Financial and Economic Crime Unit, the Cyber Crime Unit at the Swedish National Bureau of Investigation, and the Swiss Federal Prosecutor's Office, was paramount to the apprehension of the defendants.

This case is being jointly prosecuted by the U.S. Attorney's Office for the Southern District of New York and AFMLS. The investigation and prosecution of Liberty Reserve is also supported by the Department of Justice's Office of International Affairs and Computer Crime and Intellectual Property Section. Over $40 million in assets, located in numerous countries, have been identified and placed under restraint pending forfeiture, and over 30 Liberty Reserve exchanger domain names have been seized.

Western Express

Western Express International, Inc. was a Manhattan corporation that serviced Eastern European criminals and supported global cybercrime by, among other crimes, acting as a digital currency exchanger, illegal money transmitter, and money launderer. Western Express exchanged conventional currency to e-Gold and WebMoney. It was one of the largest digital currency exchangers to operate within the United States. In total, Western Express exchanged $15 million in WebMoney and $20 million in e-Gold, which supported the global trafficking of stolen account data. To date, sixteen individuals have been found guilty through this case, including three citizens of Eastern European countries who were arrested and extradited with the assistance of the Czech Republic and Greece, with the assistance of the Department of Justice's Office of International Affairs.

This investigation was conducted jointly by the Secret Service and the Manhattan (New York County) District Attorney's Office and was successfully prosecuted by the Manhattan District Attorney's Office. The corporation and its officers ultimately pleaded guilty to laundering about $2 million dollars in connection with the scheme.

Nine of Western Express' customers were convicted by guilty plea in the conspiracy, which trafficked nearly 100,000 stolen credit card numbers and was responsible for identity theft resulting in losses of more than $5 million. After a two-and-a-half month jury trial, completed this past June, the remaining three defendants were convicted of every count. This case demonstrates how digital currency has allowed criminals around the globe to do their criminal business together while cloaked in anonymity, and despite never meeting each other in person.

Challenges Posed by Digital Currencies

The growing criminal use of digital currencies challenges the effectiveness of U.S. laws and regulations intended to limit the ability of criminals to profit from their illicit activities and move their criminal proceeds. The key U.S. laws that typically pertain to Secret Service investigations involving the illicit administration or exchange of digital currencies include the Bank Secrecy Act of 1970, the Money Laundering Suppression Act of 1994, and Title III of the USA PATRIOT Act of 2001, and associated Federal regulations. The ability of the Secret Service and other agencies to enforce current laws and regulations to suppress the use of financial systems by criminal enterprises is complicated by the increasingly transnational nature of the criminal organizations and their continued efforts to circumvent these legal controls.

Digital currencies are particularly well-suited for supporting crime that is transnational in nature, thus requiring close international partnership to conduct investigations, make arrests, and seize criminal assets. Fostering these partnerships and conducting these transnational investigations requires continual investment to maintain effective international law enforcement collaborations, and constant efforts to harmonize anti-money laundering laws and regulations.

Investigating crimes involving digital currencies and the transnational organized cyber criminals that use them also requires highly skilled criminal investigators. Hiring, developing, and retaining these special agents is a high priority for the Secret Service, but is challenging in the present fiscal environment.

Additionally, while digital currencies may support the activities of transnational criminals who prey upon Americans, the administrators and exchangers of digital currencies are often based in other countries in an effort to minimize their exposure to U.S. regulation and law enforcement.

CONCLUSION

Digital currencies have the potential to support more efficient and transparent global commerce. However, because digital currencies continue to be used to facilitate illicit activity as well, law enforcement must continually adapt their investigative tools and techniques to dismantle criminal groups that use digital currencies for fraudulent activity or money laundering. Chairman Carper and Ranking Member Coburn, thank you for this opportunity to testify regarding the investigations conducted by the Secret Service and the lessons learned from these investigations on the evolving use of digital currencies by criminal organizations.

End Notes

[1] Digital currencies are a form of electronic money used as alternate currencies. Currently no digital currency serves as legal tender or administered by a national government or central bank; as such digital currencies are a subset of virtual currencies.

[2] ICE/HSI is an investigatory arm of DHS with the jurisdiction and authority to investigate violations involving the illicit importation and exportation of merchandise, bulk cash smuggling, and financial crimes involving a nexus to the border.

[3] Section 105 of the USA PATRIOT Act of 2001 directed the Secret Service to establish a "a national network of electronic crimes task forces, ... for the purpose of preventing, detecting, and investigating various forms of electronic crimes, including potential terrorist attacks against critical infrastructure and financial payment systems." The first Secret Service ECTF was established in New York in 1995; today the Secret Service operates 33 ECTFs, as part of an expanding international network that partners Federal, state, and local law enforcement with the private sector and academia to effectively investigate cyber and cyber-related crimes.

[4] FinCEN defines "virtual currency" as those currencies that operates like currency in some environments, but does not have legal tender status in any jurisdiction. Department of Treasury Financial Crimes Enforcement Network, Guidance FIN-2013-G0001 "Application of FinCEN's Regulations to Persons Administrating, Exchanging, or using Virtual Currencies" (March 18, 2013).

[5] Most notably 18 U.S.C. §§ 1028, 1029, 1030, 1343, 1956, 1960, et al.

[6] Liberty Reserve is currently under prosecution, the information in this section is based on the documents released by Department of Justice at: http://www.justice.gov/usao/nys/pressreleases/May13/LibertyReserveetalDocuments.php.

[7] Other estimates of the total volume of transactions and money laundered are substantially higher.

In: Virtual Currency …
Editor: Valerie Duskin
ISBN: 978-1-63117-280-9

Chapter 5

TESTIMONY OF PATRICK MURCK, GENERAL COUNSEL, THE BITCOIN FOUNDATION. HEARING ON "BEYOND SILK ROAD: POTENTIAL RISKS, THREATS, AND PROMISES OF VIRTUAL CURRENCIES"*

EXECUTIVE SUMMARY

Bitcoin is a decentralized store of value and open-ledger payment network that operates securely, efficiently, and at low cost without the need for any third-party intermediaries. The Bitcoin protocol allows individuals or service providers access to a global financial system that will see rapid innovation.

Bitcoin and digital currency alone will not alleviate issues of poverty and financial exclusion that effect vulnerable populations around the world. However, Bitcoin can provide a safe store of wealth and a global transaction network that cannot be corrupted or abused by those who would seek to exploit or harm vulnerable populations. It can help advance liberty and dignity for people worldwide, restore financial privacy for law-abiding people, and provide a stable money supply in countries where the currency may be mismanaged.

The United States has an acute interest in maintaining its place as a global leader in developing this cutting edge technology, fostering financial services

* This is an edited, reformatted and augmented version of a testimony, presented November 18, 2013 before the Senate Committee on Homeland Security and Governmental Affairs.

innovation, and spreading individual freedom and liberty around the globe. Applying consistent rules and regulations that encourage technological experimentation is critical to a vibrant entrepreneurial community, and this committee's work may help to chart a safe and sane regulatory course for the digital economy in general and Bitcoin specifically.

Though challenges exist, Bitcoin does not pose a unique or unsolvable challenge to law enforcement or existing regulatory structures. Bitcoin service providers enter a highly regulated marketplace with deeply entrenched competitors.

The Bitcoin Foundation looks forward to continuing a dialog with this committee and others, federal and state regulators, law enforcement agencies, financial services firms and banks, and academics. Together, we can help ensure that the substantial benefits of the digital economy are attained while the risks are mitigated.

INTRODUCTION

Good afternoon, Chairman Carper, Ranking Member Coburn, and Distinguished Members of the Committee. I am pleased to have the opportunity to speak with you today. My name is Patrick Murck, and I am general counsel of the Bitcoin Foundation.

The Bitcoin Foundation is a member-driven non-profit organization dedicated to serving the business, technology, government relations, and public affairs needs of the Bitcoin community. The Foundation works to standardize and strengthen the Bitcoin protocol and software, to protect the Bitcoin community, and to broaden the use of Bitcoin through public education and by fostering a safe and sane legal and regulatory environment. Incorporated in July of 2012, the foundation is organized under section 501(c)(6) of the Internal Revenue Code.

The Bitcoin Foundation's members include many of the top companies, entrepreneurs, and technologists working to make Bitcoin a success. The Bitcoin Foundation represents an international membership and our focus is global. Currently, about 60% of the foundation s membership is international. The rapid development of Bitcoin is a global phenomenon, and the Bitcoin 2014 conference, successor to our hugely successful Bitcoin 2013 conference in San Jose, California, earlier this year, will be held in Holland May 15-17, 2014. The Bitcoin Foundation is actively developing systems to empower local foundation subsidiaries and chapters in countries around the world with the resources they need to further the Foundation s mission of promoting, protecting and standardizing the Bitcoin protocol and distributed, decentralized digital currency in general.

I am a founding member of the Bitcoin Foundation and have served as General Counsel since its inception. Additionally, I have been an executive in legal and business development for a number of digital currency companies. In private practice, I have represented digital currency clients, and worked as a telecom, media, and technology attorney with a Washington, D.C.- based law firm. I am a native of Washington, D.C., and received my undergraduate degree from American University and my J.D. with honors from Catholic University, Columbus School of Law.

About Bitcoin

Bitcoin was invented in 2008 as a peer-to-peer payment system for use in online transactions.[1] Bitcoin is revolutionary in that, unlike any prior online payment system, Bitcoin is not administered by any central authority. There is no middleman between the sender/buyer and the receiver/seller as there is with, for example, PayPal, traditional payment cards, bank wires, or other payment systems. Bitcoin is thus referred to as a decentralized digital currency.

The Bitcoin software is also open-source and non-proprietary, developed by a community of volunteers in collaboration with our Chief Scientist, Gavin Andresen. There is no Bitcoin company that manages or controls the software or its operation. If the Bitcoin Foundation ceased work on Bitcoin s technical development, the technical development work would continue among the volunteers worldwide who already do so much of the heavy lifting. If the Bitcoin Foundation or any other actor tried to take control of the Bitcoin software, the Bitcoin community would reject that and develop the software on its own, independent of such an interloper.

Instead of a central authority, the Bitcoin transaction network consists of computers around the world running the Bitcoin software, which operates the protocol for administering Bitcoin transactions. That software can be downloaded and run by anyone, and any computer running the software can join the network. Each computer on the network also maintains a copy of the universal public ledger known as the block chain.

The Block Chain

The public ledger is crucial to understand. The heart of the Bitcoin technology is this ledger that records all transactions occurring in the system. The ledger is broken into blocks of transactions, and each new block of transactions is linked to the previous block, forming what is called the block chain. The newest block at the end of the chain links back to every block that precedes it. Having access to the most recent block allows one to follow the chain backward to observe every Bitcoin transaction ever made.

New blocks are created by mining. Mining is done by solving a very difficult math problem, which creates the next block incorporating recent transactions. This is costly in terms of computer processing (hardware, electricity, and time). But though the problem is difficult to solve, the solution is easy to verify, so a miner discovering the solution can declare it (Eureka!), and nodes across the network will promptly confirm the new block.

The difficulty of the math problem increases with the amount of effort going into mining across the network. This controls the pace at which new bitcoins are added to the system, and it reduces the chance that any one miner or group will take control of the block chain. The amount of Bitcoin created by mining will drop over time until it ceases altogether in 2140 at just fewer than 21 million bitcoins in existence. In the meantime, mining will increasingly be rewarded by transaction fees.

Critically, the universal ledger prevents anyone from spending the bitcoins they own twice. Because a record of every transaction is available to all, attempts to spend the same bitcoin after it has already been transferred are easily detected using the block chain. This allows there to be purely digital transactions without any central administrator, who would otherwise manage the ledger and police against double spending of a digital currency.

How a Bitcoin Transaction Works

Any Bitcoin user can transact directly with any other Bitcoin user. To utilize the Bitcoin network, a user needs a Bitcoin address, or wallet. A Bitcoin wallet takes the form of a cryptographic public key, which is a string of numbers and letters roughly 33 digits long. Each public key has a matching private key, known only to the user.

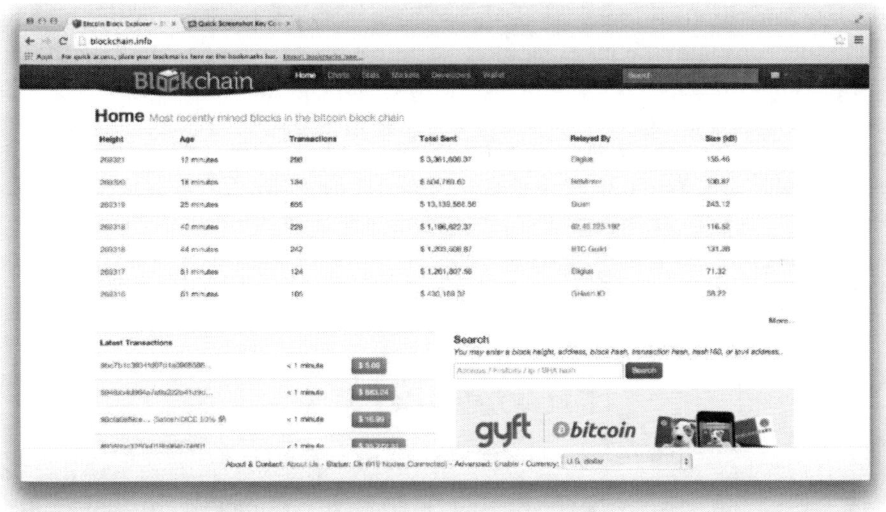

Source: blockchain.info.

Control of the private keys is what assures one of control of the bitcoins at any Bitcoin address, so collections of private keys must be protected by passwords or other means of securing them. While wallets can be created and maintained using the Bitcoin open-source software, in practice many users have accounts with one or more Bitcoin service providers and store bitcoins at addresses provided through their accounts. To initiate a transaction, the software or service sends a message to the other computers on the network announcing the transfer of a certain value in bitcoins from the user's public key to the recipient's public key. The sending user's private key is used to sign the transaction. The private key is mathematically paired with the public key, and through a standard cryptographic process of the sort used to secure website connections, every computer on the network can verify that the transaction is signed with the correct private key. The private key signature thus serves to confirm that the transaction originated with, and was approved by, the actual owner of the originating public key, and therefore that the transaction is valid.

While this process sounds complicated, it is handled automatically and invisibly for users by the Bitcoin software. From the user's perspective, sending bitcoins to someone else is no more difficult than sending funds using PayPal or traditional payment systems, or sending an email. Administering a payment or money system is not the only use of a universal public ledger. The Bitcoin protocol may expand over time to facilitate many advanced services such as deposits, escrows, and potentially even distributed stock trading. And the Bitcoin protocol may find many uses beyond payments and money, including proving the existence of documents, establishing and verifying human identities, Internet naming and numbering, and many more.

Bitcoin is a protocol. It is like TCP/IP, which enables all the different uses people around the globe invented for the Internet. And it is like HTML, which enables all the different uses people invented for the World Wide Web without having to ask anyone s permission. We envision Bitcoin as a driver of global change that rivals these other protocols in terms of the benefits it delivers to humankind across the globe.

BITCOIN'S PROMISE

There may be as many reasons to support Bitcoin as there are Bitcoin supporters. But we believe Bitcoin holds out a number of powerfully beneficial social and economic outcomes, including global financial inclusion, enhanced personal liberty and dignity, improved financial privacy, and a stable money supply for people in countries where monetary instability may threaten prosperity and even peace.

GLOBAL FINANCIAL INCLUSION

In April 2012, a World Bank report found that half of adults worldwide are unbanked due to barriers such as high cost, physical distance, and lack of proper documentation.[2] It is hard to believe amid the relative wealth of the United States, but half the world s population lacks access to financial services that are everyday matters to us. These are rungs on the ladder from poverty to prosperity that many people cannot access at all.

A 2001 study confirms in striking terms what common sense suggests: Informal saving methods such as keeping physical money in the home are subject to losses as high as 26% of the amounts saved per year.[3] Around the world, multitudes of hard-working, capable people simply lose wealth that they could use for food, shelter, medical care, and the education of their children because of underdeveloped financial infrastructure.

Bitcoin is an extremely lightweight financial infrastructure because it can exist wherever there is Internet or cell phone access and the requisite computing device, smartphone, or SMS-capable phone. Whether it brings people into existing financial services systems, or if it secures people s wealth better outside of formal systems, we believe Bitcoin has tremendous potential to improve the capacity of people around the world to build and store wealth. That greater access to wealth may produce improved outcomes in the area of food and nutrition, health and longevity, education and child development, family structure, protection of civil and political rights, and even political stability and global security.

It would be a mistake, of course, to think that Bitcoin can simply be sprinkled on longstanding social, economic, and political problems to easily solve them. And it will take time and effort to propagate the infrastructure that is needed to access and use Bitcoin in the far corners of the globe. But the Bitcoin Foundation will be fostering businesses and business environments that allow local merchants everywhere to accept bitcoins and that allow convertibility of Bitcoin to local currencies.

We believe Bitcoin can improve the lot of the world s poor. If these efforts and the underlying genius of the Bitcoin protocol improve the financial situation and wherewithal of millions, hundreds of millions, or perhaps billions of people by even a small fraction, the total quantum of good done by Bitcoin will be quite large.

Liberty and Dignity

Along similar lines, we see potential for Bitcoin to improve people s enjoyment of autonomy, liberty, and dignity everywhere in the world.

Deep running principles in Western thought, at least emphasize individuals ownership of themselves and the things they produce. In varying degrees around the world, though, governments and powerful private actors often encroach on people s rights and their ability to use and dispose of their property as they see fit. This makes people objects of control, denying them the dignity of being autonomous, independent, and responsible moral actors whose wellbeing and self-worth rise or fall based on their own decisions.

Bitcoin can facilitate private and anonymous transactions, which are resistant to oversight and control. Because it can aid people in deploying their property less subject to external impediments, Bitcoin may expand the realm of autonomy, liberty, and dignity for people around the world. This means traveling from market to village without being robbed, it means avoiding official corruption and confiscatory tax regimes, and many more things. It also means that people using Bitcoin can fund controversial speech or causes that governments and powerful private actors may seek to suppress using their control of conventional financial services. Bitcoin is a communications protocol, and it has the Internet virtue of being censorship-resistant, which expands freedom of speech and freedom of action.

This by no means implies that using Bitcoin can or should provide anyone immunity from the law. Though it has sometimes been portrayed as such in careless media stories, Bitcoin is not a magic cloaking device that allows criminal actors free reign. It does offer enhanced privacy protections, however, which is the just desert of hundreds of millions of law-abiding Americans and billions of law-abiding people worldwide.

FINANCIAL PRIVACY

The American people have been reminded this year of reasons to be concerned for their privacy, as have people around the world. We believe that peaceful, law-abiding people are entitled to protections for their privacy.

In the United States, constitutional protections such as the Fourth Amendment should allow people to be secure against unreasonable searches and seizures of their persons, houses, papers, and effects, even when their papers and effects are in digital form. We also believe the International Covenant on Civil and Political Rights bars arbitrary or unlawful interference with one s privacy, family, home, or correspondence, regardless of format.

Privacy is many things to many people. Among other things, it is the individual s bulwark against objectification by governments, corporations, and other individuals. People who have their privacy have more personal power and a richer, more independent life. Privacy is also a means to various ends, including personal security and freedom of speech and action.

Many at the Bitcoin Foundation and in the Bitcoin community are acutely aware that financial transactions in nearly every format are subject to some degree of surveillance. For good and bad, centralized payment systems always include gatekeepers and overseers. Bitcoin can facilitate fully private transactions, which, when legal in the jurisdictions where they occur, are nobody s business but the parties to the transactions.

Privacy can mask wrongful behavior, of course, and governments have a valid interest in information about activities they have made illegal. And there are certainly circumstances when Bitcoin-based services will require and benefit from collection of personal information about users. So more privacy is not the essence of Bitcoin. But the use of Bitcoin should strengthen the hand of individual users to protect their privacy.

Today, privacy in financial services is typically dictated by governments and corporations. The bitcoin ecosystem should be more amenable to what we refer to as user-defined privacy. Bitcoin may once again allow law-abiding people to have privacy on the terms they want it.

STABLE MONEY SUPPLY

A significant benefit of Bitcoin in the eyes of many in the Bitcoin community is its assurance of a stable base money supply. As I noted earlier, the bitcoin protocol provides for mining of a limited number of bitcoins, and that limit cannot be changed without the consensus of the community. The production of bitcoins will slow according to a schedule until around 2140, when the last new fraction of a bitcoin, known as a satoshi, will be mined just shy of 21 million bitcoins.

The rate of new bitcoin mining is similar to the mining rate of precious metals such as gold or silver. A low rate of new creation relative to the existing base means that added supply does not significantly debase the value of the existing stock. Like these precious metals and unlike fiat currencies, the stock of Bitcoin cannot increase rapidly, causing them to drop in value relative to other goods.

This means that Bitcoin is largely inflation-proof. Time and experience may prove it to be a more stable store of value than many fiat currencies, while it enjoys advantages over precious metals in other respects, such as transferability, divisibility, security in storage, and so on. This makes Bitcoin a potential key to financial well-being for savers and investors worldwide, but particularly in those jurisdictions where fiat currencies may be mismanaged.

Some Bitcoin enthusiasts may crow about the idea of Bitcoin replacing national fiat currencies, and it may be possible in a small country sometime in the future. The way to contemplate Bitcoin in the near term is as a means of making a small central bank or currency bloc accountable if they poorly manage their portfolio, while at the same time ameliorating the economic effects of the central bank s mismanagement. We believe all the world s currency systems are safer if there is a more diverse web of monetary systems with which to work. We believe that Bitcoin can add to monetary stability both directly, by acting as stable money itself, and indirectly, by husbanding the behavior of central bankers.

We are very motivated at the Bitcoin Foundation by the social and economic benefits that we believe Bitcoin has to offer. We are mindful, of course, that Bitcoin is subject to misuse. It would be regrettable if the many benefits Bitcoin offers were denied the world s people, or even delayed, by overreaction to the challenges that come with this emerging new technology. We share your opinion, Chairman Carper, stated very well in a recent press release, that we need to develop thoughtful, nimble and sensible federal policies that protect the public without stifling innovation and economic growth.

BEYOND SILK ROAD

As you are likely aware, federal law enforcement recently seized the "Silk Road" website and arrested its alleged controller, Ross Ulbricht. With Silk Road shuttered, it is clear that Bitcoin thrives irrespective of sensationalist stories about a dark web of illicit transactions. Silk Road drew attention to Bitcoin, and the attention may have helped Bitcoin go mainstream, but now that it is mainstream, Bitcoin is beyond Silk Road.

Bitcoin and tools like Tor, which the U.S. Navy invented to secure the communications of ships, and which protects journalists and dissidents around the world, can be used for illicit purposes. But, as the Silk Road case makes evident, Bitcoin is not a magic cloak for illicit transactions. Bitcoin is a new and advanced technology, and law enforcement will likely have to develop new methodologies for interdicting and investigating criminal activity. This does not make it harder for law enforcement to do its important job. It simply means that law enforcement will have to learn this protocol and adjust its methods somewhat, something that has been successfully accomplished in many different contexts before.

In any event, the choice for policymakers is not whether Bitcoin will exist, and it is not whether Bitcoin will be used in the United States. The question is whether Bitcoin businesses will be integrated with the U.S. financial services system and become producers of U.S. jobs and economic growth that respond to legitimate U.S. law enforcement inquiries, or whether Bitcoin businesses will move offshore, taking jobs and innovation with them, and making it harder for U.S. law enforcement to gather information for legitimate investigations.

TRUE: BITCOIN CAN BE USED FOR ILLICIT PURPOSES, LIKE ALL OTHER FORMS OF PAYMENT

Bitcoin is no different than any other payment system, form of money, or technical infrastructure. It can be used by criminals. Bitcoin was used on the Silk Road website, which was primarily a market for illegal drugs. The less this colors public and policymaker assessments of Bitcoin, the better. Criminals do turn the beneficial instruments of society to their ends. But overreacting to this simple and obvious fact because Bitcoin is exotic and new could delay Americans enjoyment of Bitcoin s benefits, which are vastly greater than its potential costs.

An analysis by digital currency research and data site *The Genesis Block* puts the relationship between Silk Road and Bitcoin in perspective. In a thoroughly researched October 2013 piece entitled, Analysis of Silk Road s Historical Impact on Bitcoin, writer Jonathan Stacke finds that a significant portion of bitcoin s early traction and price gains can be traced directly to Silk Road, with that impact waning over time, most dramatically in the past six months. [4]

In late December 2010 and early 2011, Stacke finds, people acquiring bitcoin for use on Silk Road may have produced a spike in Bitcoin s price against the U.S. dollar from $0.30 to a trading range of $0.65 to $0.80. Mainstream press attention from *The New York Times*, *Time*, and Gawker.com then began a far more significant price spike that reached $30 per Bitcoin before prices settled to a new higher equilibrium of around $5. Succeeding price changes, Stacke finds, correlate to events and news reporting unrelated to Silk Road. But denial-ofservice attacks on Silk Road in April and May of 2012 show effects falling to between 25% and 35% of Bitcoin s price. When Silk Road was finally taken down last month, the price of Bitcoin suffered a one-day drop of about 20%, but then began climbing relentlessly, more than doubling since then.

The Bitcoin market is infinitesimal compared to its potential size, so it is subject to relatively high volatility. That volatility will drop over time, as the worldwide use of the Bitcoin protocol grows. Psychology around this new asset probably also drives wider price swings than will occur in the future. But judging by their behavior in the markets, the Bitcoin community seems relieved and optimistic about the falling relevance of Silk Road and illicit markets.

As with every other payment system, criminals will surely and regrettably use bitcoins. That said, law enforcement appears well-equipped to deal with copycat sites to Silk Road. In fact, copycats Atlantis and Project Black Flag have recently shuttered themselves spontaneously and absconded with their users bitcoins. Criminals are not reliable business partners, and they will turn on each other when the circumstances are right. Anonymity is also a two-way street. A top dealer on Silk Road was actively working with federal law enforcement, the anonymity of Silk Road making it easier for them to make undercover drug deals and subsequent arrests. A user of Black Market Reloaded, another Silk Road copycat, was recently arrested.

The document charging Ross Ulbricht noted Bitcoin s legitimate uses, and it shows that solid law enforcement work is effective with respect to Bitcoin and Tor just like other payment and communications systems. Silk Road is gone. The lawful uses of Bitcoin will continue to grow in number and quantity, easily swamping illicit uses and helping to bring the association between Bitcoin and crime into accurate perspective.

New, Not Necessarily Harder

As I said earlier, Bitcoin is not a magic cloak for illicit transactions. At the same time, it certainly may provide new challenges to law enforcement, who will have to learn about Bitcoin and the block chain to pursue investigations. But we expect the law enforcement challenge to be different, not necessarily harder, in the Bitcoin environment. Law enforcement has and will be able to successfully investigate and prosecute criminals who use bitcoins.

We see the law enforcement paradigm in the Bitcoin ecosystem differing from the status quo in the following way: Law enforcement investigations using payment systems today typically are "parties known/transactions unknown." Having some insight into suspected criminal behavior, law enforcers use warrants, subpoenas, and other legitimate investigative tools to learn from financial services providers what transactions their suspects have engaged in.

If Bitcoin businesses thrive in the United States, investigations may still follow this model, gathering the Bitcoin transactions of existing suspects from U.S.-based providers. But investigations may also follow a "transaction known/parties unknown" model. The block chain that worldwide public ledger of all transactions may permit law enforcement to observe transaction flows that they know to be illicit or to use the products of illicit activity. Tracing illicit transactions to transactions that identify the parties will reveal the identities of suspects.

The block chain may be so revealing that the problem with Bitcoin is the difficulty law-abiding people have maintaining privacy. Bitcoin mixing services, which are intended to obscure the source of their users bitcoins, may become popular if the sense of the Bitcoin community is that the flow of bitcoins is being used for excessive or illegitimate surveillance of private financial activity. Incautious behavior on the part of governments and law enforcement could make the Bitcoin environment harder to work with.

The issues here are complex, and the capacity of mixing services to truly obscure transaction flow will be the subject of much study over time. But a cautious law enforcement approach to Bitcoin is much smarter than trying to convert the Bitcoin block chain and the data held by Bitcoin service providers into a mass surveillance system.

Nimble and sensible interaction with the Bitcoin community will permit law enforcement to protect the public without stifling innovation and economic growth. U.S. law enforcement will have better access to data sought under legitimate legal processes if the U.S. Bitcoin industry is strong. Simply put, U.S. companies will be easier to work with than overseas firms. But some circumstances are already driving Bitcoin businesses offshore.

Bitcoin and the U.S. Financial Services System

While we have been pleased by the solicitous tone of official policy statements coming from U.S. federal government agencies, some factors appear to be driving Bitcoin start-ups away from U.S. shores. To the extent this happens, it comes at the cost of innovation, jobs, and economic growth that Bitcoin promises the United States. Conditions are improving, but initial hostility to Bitcoin in some states may have unnerved U.S. financial services providers, forestalling their adoption of Bitcoin and their provision of service to Bitcoin businesses. We would like to see conditions improve.

Official Policy Recognizes Bitcoin

We have been pleased by federal regulators recognition of Bitcoin as an exciting and innovative entrant into the field of digital currency and financial services generally. Directly or indirectly a number of federal agencies have recognized Bitcoin and even touted its genius.

In March, for example, the Financial Crimes Enforcement Network (FinCEN) in the U.S. Treasury Department issued guidance on the application of money transmitter rules to Bitcoin businesses. Some interpreted this as official recognition that Bitcoin is valid and legitimate. We believe it signaled that existing regulation covers most of the business activity taking place in the Bitcoin ecosystem.

There are details on which we might quibble, and to the extent FinCEN promulgated new legislative rules, we believe they should have been issued after a notice-and-comment rulemaking. But, the Bitcoin Foundation s successful meeting with financial regulators, which FinCEN hosted in August, shows that the Treasury Department and others recognize the value of dialogue and the capacity of the Bitcoin Foundation to inform their work.

Also in August, at the urging of the Securities and Exchange Commission, a federal judge ruled that Bitcoin is a form of money also fitting the definition of a security under the Securities Exchange Act. A defendant charged with pursuing a Ponzi scheme argued that the SEC did not have jurisdiction over Bitcoin transactions. The judge struck this argument down on the basis that, just like with any other form of payment, it is illegal to use Bitcoin for fraud. This is undeniably sensible and helps to protect the Bitcoin community from similar frauds and scams that may arise in the future.

These are legal questions on which more work will have to be done. Bitcoin s differing characteristics potentially make it a different asset class than what existing regulation recognizes. But it fits well within the legal and regulatory regimes that bar frauds like the Ponzi scheme at issue in that case.

The official reception for Bitcoin among U.S. federal regulators has been essentially welcoming. Even agencies that one might assume to be antagonistic to Bitcoin acknowledge its legitimacy. The Department of Justice, for example, in its charging document for the alleged founder of the Silk Road, Ross Ulbricht, took pains to note that bitcoins are legal in and of themselves and have known legitimate uses. The Federal Reserve Bank of Chicago issued a Bitcoin primer two weeks ago in which senior economist Fran ois R. Velde called Bitcoin a remarkable conceptual and technical achievement, which may well be used by existing financial institutions.

We look forward to continuing our dialogue with policymakers and regulators at both the federal and state levels. In addition to the Bitcoin Foundation, there are several industry-led efforts underway to create standards of care and best practices for digital currency exchanges (for example, the committee to explore D.A.T.A.), transaction processing (mining in some cases), and digital currency investors. We are equally pleased to support these industry efforts.

We appreciate this committee s inquiries of federal agencies regarding their approaches to Bitcoin. Our belief, supported by the agency activities noted above, is that Bitcoin and Bitcoin businesses largely fit into existing regulatory structures. Where they may not, the framework for analysis we recommend is identifying the few gaps in public protection that Bitcoin s unique characteristics may produce and determining how best to fill them. We look forward to ongoing dialogue that your sensibly structured hearing and thoughtful public comments presage.

IMPROVING THE ENVIRONMENT FOR BITCOIN

While official federal policy as developed in the agencies seems clearly to recognize Bitcoin as an innovative source of economic growth and jobs, the early treatment of Bitcoin in some states and in the banking industry has clouded the picture of the United States as a center of innovation and business development. We are optimistic that the environment for Bitcoin in the United States will improve.

As illustration of early antipathy to Bitcoin, some states have issued subpoenas and cease-anddesist letters to Bitcoin businesses and others involved in the Bitcoin community. While most states and federal regulators seem to intuitively understand this, these harsh actions are not conducive to an open and productive dialog. One state regulator issued subpoenas to 22 Bitcoin-related businesses and went on television making unfounded statements relating Bitcoin to narcoterrorism. Irresponsible public statements like these make it more likely that legitimate Bitcoin businesses will relocate to more welcoming countries.

The Bitcoin Foundation is well prepared to respond to legal inquiries and our membership does not rely on cable television for its information, but startups and small businesses are harder-pressed to respond. They may spend much of their seed capital on lawyers responding to carelessly founded government inquests. And investors, recognizing the risks of heavy-handed government actions like this, may pull out or never materialize to invest in Bitcoin companies.

We do believe that conditions are right for improvement, and we are open to dialogue with all states, as with the federal government and its agencies, seeking to apply their laws to Bitcoin use and Bitcoin businesses. In fact, we have recently perceived a marked improvement in the tone and tenor taken by both state officials and bank executives. We are optimistic that we can generate greater understanding of the opportunity and potential for this part of the digital economy.

There are certainly risks to serving innovative small businesses, but these are matched by potential profit, and we hope that U.S. financial services providers will integrate with Bitcoin. So far, U.S. banks and other financial services providers have yet to harness Bitcoin s transformative power. As a result, most Bitcoin businesses have been started by technology experts with less experience in the intricacies of federal and state anti-money-laundering laws or know-your-customer rules. Established banks could provide expert counsel and cultivate customer relationships with these companies, and we think they should.

Indeed, banks could brand and offer Bitcoin exchange services themselves, quickly becoming the de facto leaders because of their regulatory status and supreme customer identity procedures. As it stands, a majority of people still prefer banks over trusting Apple, Google, or PayPal with sensitive data. Security at banks and financial institutions usually represents the strongest in the world among private businesses. For those individuals desiring a third-party safe-keeper for their Bitcoin balances, banks would provide several obvious advantages.

Bitcoin is a global protocol that will thrive with or without U.S. government support and with or without U.S. banks, but thoughtful policymakers and businesspeople in the U.S. should work to integrate Bitcoin and banking in the United States. Doing so will bring the benefits of Bitcoin to the United States as quickly as they reach the rest of the world. Innovation, economic growth, and jobs related to Bitcoin should be welcomed by policymakers at every governmental level in the United States.

Conclusion

The horizon is bright for Bitcoin under any circumstance. We at the Bitcoin Foundation believe that this innovative protocol can deliver financial services and improve the lot of people the world over. We see coordinate gains in liberty and human dignity, also spanning the globe. Bitcoin-based financial services can improve the privacy of law-abiding Americans and people around the world. And Bitcoin may provide a stable base money supply in countries where currency is mismanaged.

The Bitcoin story goes far beyond Silk Road. Nearly every technology has potential bad uses, but the vast majority of people are law-abiding and hard-working. In their hands, Bitcoin will produce benefits that vastly outstrip the costs of the illegal and wrongful uses.

We are pleased to report that federal agencies across the spectrum are acknowledging Bitcoin and incorporating it into their regulatory regimes. For the most part, Bitcoin fits into existing regulatory structures, and we see little need for new or changed laws, though careful assessment of regulatory gaps may reveal where the law requires tweaks to account for Bitcoin.

We see encouraging signs that early skepticism about Bitcoin in some quarters is giving way to interest and support. This bodes well for the United States because the question is not whether Bitcoin will be used here. It is how long Bitcoin s adoption will take and whether the United States will be leaders in the digital economy.

Thank you for the opportunity to share my views with you.

End Notes

[1] Satoshi Nakamoto, Bitcoin: A Peer-to-Peer Electronic Cash System, http://bitcoin.org/bitcoin.pdf.

[2] Asli Demirguc---Kunt and Leora Klapper, "Measuring Financial Inclusion: The Global Findex Database," Policy Research Working Paper No. 6025, The World Bank, Development Research Group, Finance and Private Sector Development Team (April 2012) http://www---wds.worldbank.org/servlet/WDSContentServer/WDSP/IB/2012/04/19/000158349_20120419083611/Ren dered/PDF/WPS6025.pdf.

[3] Graham A.N. Wright and Leonard Mutesasira, "The Relative Risks to the Savings of Poor People," MicroSave (January 2001) http://www.microfinancegateway.org/gm/document---1.9.28889/26216_file_The_Relative_Risks_.pdf.

[4] Jonathan Stacke, "Analysis of Silk Road's Historical Impact on Bitcoin," The Genesis Block, http://thegenesisblock.com/analysis---silk---roads---historical---impact---bitcoin/.

In: Virtual Currency …
Editor: Valerie Duskin
ISBN: 978-1-63117-280-9

Chapter 6

TESTIMONY OF JEREMY ALLAIRE, CHAIRMAN AND CEO, CIRCLE INTERNET FINANCIAL. HEARING ON "BEYOND SILK ROAD: POTENTIAL RISKS, THREATS, AND PROMISES OF VIRTUAL CURRENCIES"*

INTRODUCTION

Chairman Carper, Ranking Member Coburn and members of the Committee, my name is Jeremy Allaire and I am the Founder and CEO of Circle Internet Financial, a recently launched financial services company aimed at facilitating payments and money transfers using global digital currency such as Bitcoin. I have been building Internet software platforms and online service companies for twenty years, having founded and helped to lead multiple global public companies. The products that I have conceived and helped to build include software and online services used by hundreds of millions of consumers and hundreds of thousands of businesses around the world.

I am here to testify because I believe that global digital currency represents one of the most important technical and economic innovations of our time. Specifically, digital currency introduces advancements in electronic payments and money transfers, potentially materially lowering costs for

* This is an edited, reformatted and augmented version of a testimony, presented November 18, 2013 before the Senate Committee on Homeland Security and Governmental Affairs.

businesses around the world, decreasing fraud risk for consumers and merchants, increasing consumer privacy and protection, and expanding the market for consumer financial products on a worldwide basis.

As this technology moves from early adopters into mainstream acceptance, it is critical in my view that Federal and State governments establish policies surrounding digital currency that uphold consumer protections associated with fraud and privacy risks, ensure that criminals and bad actors find it increasingly difficult to utilize these platforms and provide clarity to consumers and businesses that conduct business using digital currency.

THE EMERGENCE OF GLOBAL DIGITAL CURRENCY

Digital currency platforms such as Bitcoin have emerged over the past several years, fostered by a number of significant technical and social advancements, including:

- Continued and broad based adoption of the Internet on a worldwide basis, which has enabled billions of consumers to instantly connect and interact anywhere and anytime.
- Dramatic growth in the adoption of smartphones and mobile devices, now used by nearly 4 billion people, and which enable digital payment applications to be available ubiquitously.
- Advances in distributed and peer-to-peer computing that enable highly efficient, global and low-cost systems and infrastructure, enabling decentralized systems of finance.
- Advances in cryptography and digital signature technology, which provide a tremendous foundation for establishing trust, security and privacy in financial transactions.
- Accelerating globalization of trade and labor, which is driving demand for more efficient, secure and cost-effective cross-border payments.

Finally, it seems clear to me that the global financial crisis shattered the trust of many consumers and businesses around the world. It should not be surprising to anyone that in the midst of what appeared to be an emerging global depression in late 2008 that innovative mathematicians, cryptography experts, and computer scientists designed a system, Bitcoin with the goal of providing a resilient yet decentralized platform for finance.

OPEN INTERNET PLATFORMS AND GLOBAL ECONOMIC INNOVATION

To put all of this in context, I think it's critical to look at the role of the Internet and open platforms in transforming industries and fostering global economic innovation. Today, open Internet-based platforms are at the center of global economic innovation in industries ranging from communications, to media, software, education, commerce and retail. However, for a variety of reasons, the technologies and business models surrounding finance have been relatively insulated from these changes over the past twenty years. Open standards, protocols and formats based on digital currency, and Bitcoin specifically, present an opportunity to transform finance to the same degree that these other industries have been transformed. Indeed, the intense globalization that we are experiencing because of the Internet is in many ways calling out for more efficient forms of currency, trade and payments than existing institutions provide.

THE NEED FOR INNOVATION IN BANKING AND FINANCE

I don't think there is much debate that we need to see innovation and transformation in banking and finance, and that on a global level we need to be thinking about what new platforms and rules of the road are needed to meet the global economic challenges that we face. Specifically, our payments systems are cumbersome and inefficient, and very much built upon systems and processes that are decades old. The result is that consumers and businesses all around the world are paying an implicit tax in the form of higher costs, lower margins and less efficient economic interaction. And, in many cases, our financial systems have excluded enormous bases of consumers who remain un-banked or under-banked.

The combination of ubiquitous Internet-connected mobile devices and digital currency presents a tremendous opportunity to radically expand access to financial services on a worldwide basis.

Payments and money transfers are still operating in the pre-internet era. Today, we can communicate freely and instantly with nearly any human on the planet; we have nearly free and instantaneous access to enormous volumes of human knowledge; we have access to — and collectively create — more media and content than was ever thought possible, also at essentially no cost. Yet, to send money between friends and family, whether across the table or across the planet, it takes days and costs a significant amount in transaction fees. Our cash-based currency systems are very costly to operate and are easily subject to abuse by criminals and money launderers. To make payments, merchants must bear significant fraud risk, consumer privacy is threatened, and likewise it takes days for a merchant to actually receive money from an electronic payment, not to mention the widely perceived high costs of transaction fees. The costs and complexities rise as we look at these issues on a global basis.

How Circle Is Building on This Innovation

I founded Circle with a vision that open Internet platforms for digital currency could transform and improve financial products to the same degree that Internet platforms have transformed media, communications, commerce, education and so many other industries. Specifically, we are building online services for consumers and businesses to be able to easily use digital currency, and specifically Bitcoin, to send and receive money and make and accept payments. For consumers, we intend to enable them to easily purchase, store, send, receive and make payments using Bitcoin, and for businesses we are providing tools to help them easily accept digital currency payments.

We are fully committed to complying with all applicable laws and regulations and establishing comprehensive risk management protocols. In particular, recognizing that we are subject to regulation as a money services business, we have registered with FinCEN as a money transmitter, and are actively seeking licenses from U.S. State financial authorities to operate as a money transmitter within their jurisdictions. We are developing our platforms to provide very high levels of security for our users, and employing industry-leading approaches to customer identity verification, fraud remediation and anti-money laundering, including a BSA/AML/OFAC compliance program, designed in partnership with leading regulatory advisors and experts.

Risks and Threats Created by Global Digital Currency

As digital currency gains more traction, U.S. regulators and law enforcement are justifiably focused on the potential use of digital currencies to finance criminal activities, including terrorism. As evidenced by Silk Road, and other recent legal and enforcement actions, digital currency, just like cash, can indeed be used for nefarious means. Silk Road also demonstrates the importance of industry players implementing robust fraud and anti-money laundering programs and working closely with law enforcement to prevent and report this type of behavior.

A number of potential risks exist with digital currency that need to be considered by government, including:

- Criminals and terrorists will seek to employ digital currency if it remains unregulated, leaving Bitcoin operators to operate without stringent controls and effective systems to verify identities, monitor transactions, and report suspicious activity.
- Tax cheaters will seek to employ digital currency to evade taxes if the government doesn't issue and enforce clear guidelines and rules on the role of digital currency in accounting for income and taxation in U.S. Dollars, and businesses will be uncertain as to how to account for revenue and income received in digital currency.
- Consumers and businesses could be defrauded if Bitcoin operators are allowed to operate without the highest levels of security when storing digital currency and associated personal information.
- Consumers and businesses could be exposed to financial loss if Bitcoin market prices fluctuate wildly, and central banks and institutional investors are not able to act as market-makers in Bitcoin.
- Because Bitcoin is not centrally controlled and relies upon an open network of computing nodes that provide transaction processing and payment confirmations while securing the network as a whole, it is potentially subject to malicious "51% attacks" that aim to disrupt Bitcoin's records of asset ownership.

At Circle, we are committed to working with key government agencies and policy makers to ensure safeguards are in place to mitigate these risks. These safeguards include the development of strong Know Your Customer

("KYC") standards for customers and counterparties, transaction monitoring, and regulatory reporting. We are encouraged by the ongoing dialogue and the formation of groups, such as the Bitcoin Foundation and the Digital Asset Transfer Authority ("DATA"), which are coordinating to develop best practices within the industry.

GOVERNMENT AND REGULATORY REGIMES NEEDED FOR DIGITAL CURRENCY

All of these risks and opportunities require that governments around the world take a proactive stance with regards to guidance around digital currency. It should be noted that digital currency has expanded globally due to different regulatory standards and attitudes overseas, particularly in the European Union and China. Several foreign firms have also refused to accept U.S. customers due to the lack of clear regulatory guidance. We do not think that it is in anyone's best interest for digital currency to become an offshore industry, or an industry dominated by China. No other country in the world has a startup entrepreneurial culture like the United States. We should protect and embolden this spirit that creates economic growth and provides us with a considerable global advantage.

In terms of U.S. regulation, it appears to me that Federal and State regulators generally appear to have ample statutory authority to adopt regulations and take enforcement actions as necessary to protect consumers and ensure responsible conduct in the world of Bitcoin commerce, that their actions to date have been constructive, and that we stand ready to assist them in their ongoing efforts to adapt their regulatory tools to new digital currency.

I believe we are at the forefront of another twenty year journey of Internet-led transformation, this time in our global financial systems, and the opportunity is to foster that economic change while simultaneously putting in place the safeguards that only government can enable.

Mr. Chairman, that concludes my prepared testimony. I would be happy to answer any questions for the Committee.

In: Virtual Currency … ISBN: 978-1-63117-280-9
Editor: Valerie Duskin

Chapter 7

TESTIMONY OF JERRY BRITO, SENIOR RESEARCH FELLOW, MERCATUS CENTER AT GEORGE MASON UNIVERSITY. HEARING ON "BEYOND SILK ROAD: POTENTIAL RISKS, THREATS, AND PROMISES OF VIRTUAL CURRENCIES"*

Mr. Chairman and members of the Committee, thank you for inviting me here today to comment on the risks and promises of virtual currencies. My name is Jerry Brito and I am a senior research fellow at the Mercatus Center at George Mason University, where I study the regulation of emerging technologies in the Mercatus Center's Technology Policy Program.

We're here today to discuss virtual currencies in general, but it is Bitcoin in particular that has so many interested in this topic.

Online virtual currencies are nothing new. They have existed for decades. From World of Warcraft Gold to Face-book Credits to e-gold. Neither are online payments systems new. PayPal, Visa, and Western Union Pay are all examples. So what is it about Bitcoin and similar cryptocurrencies that makes them unique?

Whatever one may think about Bitcoin's prospects for enduring value, it is safe to say that it is a remarkable technical achievement.[1] Bitcoin is the world's first completely decentralized digital currency, and it's the decentral-

* Presented November 18, 2013 before the Senate Committee on Homeland Security and Governmental Affairs.

ized part that makes it unique. Prior to Bitcoin's invention in 2009, online currencies or payments systems had to be managed by a central authority, whether it was Facebook issuing Facebook Credits or PayPal ensuring that transactions between its customers were reconciled. However, by solving a longstanding conundrum in computer science known as the "double spend" problem, Bitcoin for the first time makes possible transactions online that are person to person, without the need for an intermediary between them, just like cash.

This technical breakthrough presents both potential benefits for consumers and the economy and challenges to law enforcement. For example, because there is no central intermediary in Bitcoin transactions, there are little to no fees associated with those transactions, which especially benefits small businesses and price-sensitive consumers. And because Bitcoin is not a proprietary platform run by a single company but an open network, entrepreneurs need no permission to experiment and innovate new products and services.

On the flip side, law enforcement has long relied on financial intermediaries to help them detect, prevent, and investigate illegal transactions. Because bitcoin transactions can have no intermediaries, and because bitcoin transactions are not necessarily tied to identities, it is not surprising that we have seen Bitcoin employed in criminal transactions. In particular, Bitcoin has been used for the sale of drugs and in malware that holds one's data hostage. It's also not difficult to imagine how the technology could be employed in money laundering.

Emerging technologies often present both great potential benefits as well as real risks. For example, 3D printing can be used to cheaply make prostheses and life-saving medical devices, but also undetectable firearms. Domestic commercial drones have the potential to revolutionize agriculture and shipping, but could also be used for stalking. The challenge for policymakers is to address the risks posed by emerging technologies while doing no harm to the innovative potential of that technology.

In many cases where emerging technologies pose risks, there will already be laws and regulations of general applicability that address many of those risks without the need for new laws targeted at the specific technology. This is the case with Bitcoin. While bitcoin transactions do not require intermediaries, one must still acquire bitcoins by exchanging dollars, and merchants that accept bitcoins will very often use Bitcoin payment processors. Indeed, there is a fast-growing ecosystem of start-up exchanges, payment processors, and wallet and escrow services that make up Bitcoin's burgeoning infrastructure.

Each of these are already subject to regulation as money transmitters, including state licensing and FinCEN registration, as well as "know your customer" and "suspicious activity report" requirements.

More to the point, serious criminals looking to hide their tracks are more likely to choose a centralized virtual currency run by an intermediary willing to lie to regulators for a fee, rather than a decentralized currency like Bitcoin that, as a technical matter, must make a record of every transaction, even if pseudonymously. While the online black market Silk Road, which used bitcoins, is estimated to have generated less than $200 million in drug sales,[2] the centralized digital currency Liberty Reserve is believed to have laundered more than $6 billion related to credit card fraud, identity theft, computer hacking, and child pornography.[3] The reason Liberty Reserve, and not Bitcoin, was the payment system of choice for criminals online is that it was designed and managed by its creators to avoid "know your customer" and reporting rules and to evade subpoena.

As a result, the path forward that can best confront risks while ensuring that we can reap Bitcoin's beneficial potential is to allow the Bitcoin network and its surrounding infrastructure to develop by making sure that entrepreneurial innovators can easily comply with existing regulation. The alternative, promulgating special regulations for virtual currencies or otherwise making it more costly to operate legitimately in the space, could have two unintended consequences. First, it might mean ceding the network to exclusively illegal use and forgoing any visibility that law enforcement could otherwise gain into the activities of compliant firms. Second, the United States could lose its head start in what may be the next disruptive industry if it establishes a regulatory regime that hampers Bitcoin while other countries, like China and Canada,[4] look for ways to develop workable regulatory frameworks for Bitcoin.

Finally, as regulatory and law enforcement agencies seek to apply existing law to Bitcoin, they will face the challenge that Bitcoin is not a company with easily identifiable executives, but instead an open-source project and a community. The Bitcoin Foundation is central to that community, but it does not encompass the whole community. So as new guidelines and procedures are developed, policymakers should make sure to engage the community and solicit comments from the public to ensure that they benefit from a wide range of perspectives.

Thank you for your time and I look forward to your questions.[5]

About the Author

Jerry Brito is a senior research fellow at the Mercatus Center at George Mason University and director of its Technology Policy Program. He also serves as an adjunct professor of law at George Mason University. His research focuses on technology and Internet policy, copyright, and the regulatory process.

About the Mercatus Center

The Mercatus Center at George Mason University is the world's premier university source for market-oriented ideas—bridging the gap between academic ideas and real-world problems.

A university-based research center, Mercatus advances knowledge about how markets work to improve people's lives by training graduate students, conducting research, and applying economics to offer solutions to society's most pressing problems.

Our mission is to generate knowledge and understanding of the institutions that affect the freedom to prosper and to find sustainable solutions that overcome the barriers preventing individuals from living free, prosperous, and peaceful lives.

Founded in 1980, the Mercatus Center is located on George Mason University's Arlington campus.

www.mercatus.org

Appendix: Bitcoin: A Primer for Policymakers

Jerry Brito[1] and Andrea Castillo[2]

Bitcoin is the world's first completely decentralized digital currency. Four short years ago, knowledge of it was confined to a handful of hobbyists on Internet forums. Today, the bitcoin economy is larger than the economies of some of the world's smaller nations. The value of a bitcoin (or BTC) has grown and fluctuated greatly, from pennies in its early days to over $390 at its peak in November 2013. The current market capitalization of the bitcoin economy is estimated to be over $4 billion.[3] Businesses big and small have shown interest in integrating the Bitcoin platform into their operations and providing new services within the bitcoin economy. Venture capitalists, too, are eager to put their money behind this growing industry.[4] Traditional financial institutions and researchers, too, have taken notice. Noting its rapid development and status as a "remarkable conceptual and technical achievement," the Federal Reserve Bank of Chicago recently released a primer on the cryptocurrency.[5] The development of Bitcoin and its early successes are an exciting testament to the ingenuity of the modern entrepreneur.

Because Bitcoin is decentralized, it can be used pseudonymously, and this has attracted the attention of regulators. The same qualities that make Bitcoin attractive as a payment system could also allow users to evade taxes, launder money, and trade illicit goods. Both the Financial Crimes Enforcement Network (FinCEN) of the US Department of the Treasury[6] and the Department of Justice[7] have released official statements regarding the regulation of virtual currencies, including Bitcoin. A Government Accountability Office report on virtual currencies urged the IRS to reduce tax-compliance risks by issuing a guidance.[8] The appendix of that report contains a letter from IRS Deputy Commissioner Steven T. Miller, who assured the office that the IRS is "working to address these risks." Additionally, a commissioner of the Commodities Futures Trading Commission recently expressed interest in exploring whether Bitcoin falls within the commission's jurisdiction.[9] In considering how to best oversee this still-nascent technology, government regulators should take care that their overlapping directives do not hinder the promising growth potential of this innovative financial platform.

This paper will provide a short introduction to the Bitcoin network, including its properties, operations, and pseudonymous character. It will describe the benefits of allowing the Bitcoin network to develop and innovate, while highlighting issues of concern for consumers, policymakers, and regulators. It will describe the current regulatory landscape and explore other potential regulations that could be promulgated. The paper will conclude by providing policy recommendations that will assuage policymakers' common concerns while allowing for innovation within the Bitcoin network.

What Is Bitcoin?

Bitcoin is an open-source, peer-to-peer digital currency. Among many other things, what makes Bitcoin unique is that it is the world's first completely decentralized digital-payments system. This may sound complicated, but the underlying concepts are not difficult to understand.

Overview

Until Bitcoin's invention in 2008 by the unidentified programmer known as Satoshi Nakamoto, online transactions always required a trusted third-party intermediary. For example, if Alice wanted to send $100 to Bob over the Internet, she would have had to rely on a third-party service like PayPal or MasterCard. Intermediaries like PayPal keep a ledger of account holders' balances. When Alice sends Bob $100, PayPal deducts the amount from her account and adds it to Bob's account.

Without such intermediaries, digital money could be spent twice. Imagine there are no intermediaries with ledgers, and digital cash is simply a computer file, just as digital documents are computer files. Alice could send $100 to Bob by attaching a money file to a message. But just as with email, sending an attachment does not remove it from one's computer. Alice would retain a copy of the money file after she had sent it. She could then easily send the *same* $100 to Charlie. In computer science, this is known as the "double-spending" problem,[10] and until Bitcoin it could only be solved by employing a ledger-keeping trusted third party.

Bitcoin's invention is revolutionary because for the first time the double-spending problem can be solved without the need for a third party. Bitcoin does this by distributing the necessary ledger among all the users of the system via a peer-to-peer network. Every transaction that occurs in the bitcoin economy is registered in a public, distributed ledger, which is called the block chain. New transactions are checked against the block chain to ensure that the same bitcoins haven't been previously spent, thus eliminating the double-spending problem. The global peer-to-peer network, composed of thousands of users, takes the place of an intermediary; Alice and Bob can transact without PayPal.

One thing to note right away is that transactions on the Bitcoin network are not denominated in dollars or euros or yen as they are on PayPal, but are instead denominated in bitcoins. This makes it a virtual currency in addition to a decentralized payments network. The value of the currency is not derived from gold or government fiat, but from the value that people assign to it.

The dollar value of a bitcoin is determined on an open market, just as is the exchange rate between different world currencies.[11]

Operation

So far we have discussed what Bitcoin is: a decentralized peer-to-peer payments network and a virtual currency that essentially operates as online cash. Now we will take a closer look at how Bitcoin works.

Transactions are verified, and double-spending is prevented, through the clever use of public-key cryptography.[12] Public-key cryptography requires that each user be assigned two "keys," one private key that is kept secret like a password, and one public key that can be shared with the world. When Alice decides to transfer bitcoins to Bob, she creates a message, called a "transaction," which contains Bob's public key, and she "signs" it with her private key. By looking at Alice's public key, anyone can verify that the transaction was indeed signed with her private key, that it is an authentic exchange, and that Bob is the new owner of the funds. The transaction—and thus the transfer of ownership of the bitcoins—is recorded, time-stamped, and displayed in one "block" of the block chain. Public-key cryptography ensures that all computers in the network have a constantly updated and *verified* record of all transactions within the Bitcoin network, which prevents double-spending and fraud.

What does it mean when we say that "the network" verifies transactions and reconciles the ledger? And how exactly are new bitcoins created and introduced into the money supply? As we have already seen, because Bitcoin is a peer-to-peer network, there is no central authority charged with either creating currency units or verifying transactions. This network depends on users who provide their computing power to do the logging and reconciling of transactions. These users are called "miners"[13] because they are rewarded for their work with newly created bitcoins. Bitcoins are created, or "mined," as thousands of dispersed computers solve complex math problems that verify the transactions in the block chain. As one commentator has put it,

> The actual mining of Bitcoins is by a purely mathematical process. A useful analogy is with the search for prime numbers: it used to be fairly easy to find the small ones (Eratosthenes in Ancient Greece produced the first algorithm for finding them). But as they were found it got harder to find the larger ones. Nowadays researchers use advanced high-performance computers to find them and their achievements are noted by the mathematical community (for example, the University of Tennessee maintains a list of the highest 5,000).
>
> For Bitcoins the search is not actually for prime numbers but to find a sequence of data (called a "block") that produces a particular pattern when the Bitcoin "hash" algorithm is applied to the data. When a match occurs the

> miner obtains a bounty of Bitcoins (and also a fee if that block was used to certify a transaction). The size of the bounty reduces as Bitcoins around the world are mined.
>
> The difficulty of the search is also increased so that it becomes computationally more difficult to find a match. These two effects combine to reduce over time the rate at which Bitcoins are produced and mimic the production rate of a commodity like gold. At some point new Bitcoins will not be produced and the only incentive for miners will be transaction fees.[14]

So, the protocol was designed so that each miner contributes a computer's processing power toward maintaining the infrastructure needed to support and authenticate the currency network. Miners are awarded newly created bitcoins for contributing their processing power toward maintaining the network and verifying transactions in the block chain. And as more processing power is dedicated to mining, the protocol will increase the difficulty of the math problem, ensuring that bitcoins are always mined at a predictable and limited rate.

This process of mining bitcoins will not continue forever. Bitcoin was designed to mimic the extraction of gold or other precious metals from the earth—only a limited, known number of bitcoins can ever be mined. The arbitrary number chosen to be the cap is 21 million bitcoins. Miners are projected to painstakingly harvest the last "satoshi," or 0.00000001 of a bitcoin, in the year 2140. If the total mining power scales to a high enough level, the difficulty in mining bitcoins will have increased so much that procuring this last satoshi will be quite a challenging digital undertaking. Once the last satoshi has been mined, miners that contribute their processing power toward verifying transactions will be rewarded through transaction fees rather than mined bitcoins. This ensures that miners still have an incentive to keep the network running after the last bitcoin is mined.

Pseudonymity

A great deal of attention given to Bitcoin in the media centers on the anonymity that the digital currency is supposed to lend its users. This idea stems from a mistaken understanding of the currency, however.

Because online transactions to date have required a third-party intermediary, they have not been anonymous. PayPal, for example, will have a record of every time Alice has sent Bob money. And because Alice's and Bob's PayPal accounts are tied to their respective bank accounts, their identities are likely known. In contrast, if Alice gives Bob a $100 bill in cash, there is no intermediary and no record of the transaction. And if Alice and Bob don't know each other's identities, we can say the transaction is completely anonymous.

Bitcoin falls somewhere between these two extremes. On the one hand, bitcoins are like cash in that once Alice gives bitcoins to Bob, she no longer has them and Bob does, and there is no third-party intermediary between them that knows their respective identities. On the other hand, unlike cash, the fact that a transaction took place between two public keys, the time, the amount, and other information is recorded in the block chain. Indeed, every transaction that has ever occurred in the history of the bitcoin economy is publicly viewable in the block chain.[15]

While the public keys for all transactions—also known as "Bitcoin addresses"[16]—are recorded in the block chain, those public keys are not tied to anyone's identity. Yet if a person's identity were linked to a public key, one could look through the recorded transactions in the block chain and easily see all transactions associated with that key. So, while Bitcoin is very similar to cash in that parties can transact without disclosing their identities to a third party or to each other, it is unlike cash in that all the transactions to and from a particular Bitcoin address can be traced. In this way Bitcoin is not anonymous, but pseudonymous.

Tying a real-world identity to a pseudonymous Bitcoin address is not as difficult as some might imagine. For one thing, a person's identity (or at least identifying information, such as an IP address) is often recorded when the person makes a Bitcoin transaction at a website, or exchanges dollars for bitcoins at a bitcoin exchange. To increase the chances of remaining pseudonymous, one would have to employ anonymizing software like Tor, and take care never to transact with Bitcoin addresses that could be tied back to one's identity.

Finally, it is also possible to glean identities simply by looking at the block chain. One study found that behavior-based clustering techniques could reveal the identities of 40 percent of Bitcoin users in their simulated Bitcoin experiment.[17] An early analysis of the statistical properties of the Bitcoin transaction graph showed how a passive network analysis with the appropriate tools can divulge the financial activity and identities of Bitcoin users.[18] A later analysis of the statistical properties of the Bitcoin transaction graph garnered similar results with a larger dataset.[19] Another analysis of the Bitcoin transaction graph reiterated that observers using "entity merging"[20] can observe structural patterns in user behavior and emphasized that this is "one of the most important challenges to Bitcoin anonymity."[21] In spite of this, Bitcoin users do enjoy a much higher level of privacy than do users of traditional digital-transfer services, who must provide detailed personal information to the third-party financial intermediaries that facilitate the exchange.

Although Bitcoin is frequently referred to as an "anonymous" currency, in reality, it is very difficult to stay anonymous in the Bitcoin network. Pseudonyms tied to transactions recorded in the public ledger can be identified years after an exchange is made. Once Bitcoin intermediaries are fully compliant with the bank-secrecy regulations required of traditional financial intermediaries, anonymity will be even less guaranteed, because Bitcoin intermediaries will be required to collect personal data on their customers.

Benefits

The first question that many people have when they learn about Bitcoin is, Why would I want to use bitcoins when I can use dollars? Bitcoin is still a new and fluctuating currency that is not accepted by many merchants, so the uses for Bitcoin may seem mostly experimental. To better understand why people might want to use Bitcoin, it helps to think of it, not necessarily as a replacement for traditional currencies, but rather as a new payments system.

Lower Transaction Costs

Because there is no third-party intermediary, Bitcoin transactions are substantially cheaper and quicker than traditional payment networks. And because transactions are cheaper, Bitcoin makes micropayments and other innovations possible. Additionally, Bitcoin holds much promise as a way to lower transaction costs for small businesses and global remittances, alleviate global poverty by improving access to capital, protect individuals against capital controls and censorship, ensure financial privacy for oppressed groups, and spur innovation (within and on top of the Bitcoin protocol). On the other hand, Bitcoin's decentralized nature also presents opportunities for crime. The challenge, then, is to develop processes that diminish the opportunities for criminality while maintaining the benefits that Bitcoin can provide.

First, Bitcoin is attractive to cost-conscious small businesses looking for ways to lower the transaction costs of doing business. Credit cards have greatly expanded the ease of transacting, but their use comes with considerable costs to merchants. Businesses that wish to offer the option of credit card payments to their customers must first pay for a merchant account with each credit card company. Depending on the terms of agreement with each credit card company, businesses must then pay a variety of authorization fees, transaction fees, statement fees, interchange fees, and customer-service fees, among other charges. These fees quickly add up and significantly increase the cost of doing business. However, if a merchant neglects to accept credit card payments to save on fees, he or she could lose a considerable amount of business from customers who enjoy the ease of credit cards.

Since Bitcoin facilitates direct transactions without a third party, it removes costly charges that accompany credit card transactions. The Founders Fund, the venture capital fund headed by Peter Thiel of PayPal and Facebook fame, recently invested $3 million in the payment-processing company BitPay because of the service's ability to lower the costs of doing online commerce across borders.[22] In fact, small businesses have already started to accept bitcoins as a way to avoid the costs of doing business with credit card companies.[23] Others have adopted the currency for its speed and efficiency in facilitating transactions.[24] Merchants labeled "high risk" by credit card companies have difficulty finding a payment processor willing to work with them, so they have turned to Bitcoin merchant services providers, like BitPay, as an affordable and convenient alternative to credit card services.[25] Bitcoin will likely continue to lower transaction costs for businesses that accept it as more people adopt the currency.

Accepting credit card payments also puts businesses on the hook for charge-back fraud.

Merchants have long been plagued by fraudulent "charge-backs," or consumer-initiated payment reversals based on a false claim that a product has not been delivered.[26] Merchants therefore can lose the payment for the item and the item itself, and also have to pay a fee for the charge-back. As a nonreversible payment system, Bitcoin eliminates the "friendly fraud" wrought by the misuse of consumer charge-backs. This can be very important for small businesses. As Dan Lee, the manager of a small bodega in Brooklyn, puts it, "[With Bitcoin], there are lower fees, and you don't have to worry about charge-backs, which is beneficial for merchants. It's better than Visa or MasterCard."[27] This property is so valuable to the business that Lee's Greene Avenue Market offers a 10% discount to customers who pay in Bitcoin.

Consumers like charge-backs, however, because that system protects them from unscrupulous merchants or merchant errors. Consumers may also enjoy other benefits that merchant-account fees help fund. Indeed, many consumers and merchants will probably stick to traditional credit card services even if Bitcoin payments become available. Still, the expanded choices in payment options would benefit people of all preferences.

Those who want the protection and perks of using a credit card can continue to do so, even if they pay a little more. Those who are more price- or privacy-conscious can use bitcoins instead. Not having to pay merchant fees means that merchants who accept Bitcoin have the option to pass the savings on to consumers. That is the business model of the Bitcoin Store,[28] which sells thousands of consumer electronics at discounted prices and only accepts bitcoins. The same Samsung Galaxy Note tablet that sells on Amazon for $779 plus shipping[29] sells at the Bitcoin Store for a mere $480.[30] In this way, Bitcoin provides more low-cost options to bargain hunters and small businesses without detracting from the traditional credit card services that some consumers prefer.

As an inexpensive funds-transfer system, Bitcoin also holds promise for the future of low-cost remittances. In 2012, immigrants to developed countries sent at least $401 billion in remittances back to relatives living in developing countries.[31] The amount of remittances is projected to increase to $515 billion by 2015.[32] Most of these remittances are sent using traditional brick-and-mortar wire services such as Western Union and MoneyGram, which charge steep fees for the service and can take several business days to transfer the funds.[33] In the first quarter of 2013, the global average fee for sending remittances was 9.05 percent.[34] In contrast, transaction fees on the Bitcoin network tend to be less than 0.0005 BTC,[35] or 1 percent of the transaction.[36] This entrepreneurial opportunity to improve money transfers has attracted investments from big-name venture capitalists.[37] Even MoneyGram and Western Union are contemplating whether to integrate Bitcoin into their business models.[38] Bitcoin allows for instantaneous, inexpensive remittances, and the reduction in the cost of global remittances for consumers could be considerable.

Potential to Combat Poverty and Oppression

Bitcoin also has the potential to improve the quality of life for the world's poorest. Improving access to basic financial services is a promising antipoverty technique.[39] According to one estimate, 64 percent of people living in developing countries lack access to these services, perhaps because it is too costly for traditional financial institutions to serve poor, rural areas.[40] Because of the impediments to developing traditional branch banking in poor areas, people in developing countries have turned to mobile banking services for their financial needs. The closed-system mobile payment service M-Pesa has been particularly successful in countries such as Kenya, Tanzania, and Afghanistan.[41] Entrepreneurs are already moving to this model; the Bitcoin wallet service Kipochi recently developed a product that allows M-Pesa users to exchange bitcoins.[42] Mobile banking services in developing countries can be further augmented by the adoption of Bitcoin.

Other Bitcoin business models seek to streamline Bitcoin use in developing economies. LocalBitcoins.com, a listing and escrow service for individual small Bitcoin traders, publicizes trader information in over 190 countries, including Bangladesh, Zimbabwe, the Democratic Republic of Congo, Pakistan, Venezuela, Romania, India, Libya, and other developing economies.[43] The Google- and YCombinator-backed service provider startup, Buttercoin, aims to spread Bitcoin use in the developing world by partnering with locally licensed exchange businesses to trade bitcoins for local currencies. By providing Bitcoin services to already-licensed companies in countries all over the world, Buttercoin can penetrate local markets without sacrificing compliance.[44] The company plans to open services in India by the end of 2013 and extend operations to six different countries in the following six months.[45]

Charities in the United States also have looked to Bitcoin as a promising way to alleviate poverty. Bitcoin's ease and affordability in transferring funds makes it an attractive option to lower operation costs for cash-strapped charities. The Bitcoin100 charity campaign has contributed Bitcoin donations to a number of causes since 2011.[46] Sean's Outpost, a homeless outreach organization located in Pensacola, Florida, has been providing meals and toiletries to Pensacola's neediest solely with bitcoins.[47] The charity's founder, Jason King, plans to open a nine acre homeless sanctuary, fittingly titled "Satoshi Forest," paid for entirely with Bitcoin.[48] According to King, Bitcoin's low costs and ease of transfer make it an ideal currency for his charity. "Anyone being able to send money to us in the world instantaneously is very valuable, and we've gotten donations from over twenty-three different countries," he explains.[49] As an open-system payment service, Bitcoin can provide low-income people in developing and developed countries alike with inexpensive access to financial services on a global scale.

Bitcoin might also provide relief to people living in countries with strict capital controls. The total number of bitcoins that can be mined is capped and cannot be manipulated. There is no central authority that can reverse transactions or prevent the exchange of bitcoins between countries. Bitcoin therefore provides an escape hatch for people who desire an alternative to their country's devalued currencies or frozen capital markets. We have already seen examples of people turning to Bitcoin to evade the harmful effects of capital controls and central-bank mismanagement. Some Argentines, for instance, have adopted Bitcoin in response to the country's dual burdens of a 25 percent inflation rate and strict capital controls.[50] Consumer confidence, too, continues to plunge in Argentina.[51] Demand for bitcoins is so strong in Argentina that one popular bitcoin exchange is planning to open an Argentine office.[52] Argentine Bitcoin use continues to surge in the face of Argentina's capital mismanagement.[53] For example, the Net Party, an Argentine political reform movement, was funded almost entirely with bitcoins. "There you can see the different: the speed of money," says founder Santiago Siri, "[Raising] the money would have taken eight weeks [using the official currency]; it took one hour with Bitcoin."[54]

Individuals in oppressive or emergency situations might also benefit from the financial privacy that Bitcoin can provide. There are many legitimate reasons why people seek privacy in their financial transactions. Spouses fleeing abusive partners need some way to discreetly spend money without being tracked. People seeking controversial health services desire financial privacy from family members, employers, and others who might judge their decisions. Recent experiences with despotic governments suggest that oppressed citizens would benefit greatly from the ability to make private transactions free from the grabbing hands of tyrants. Bitcoin provides some of the privacy that has traditionally been afforded through cash—with the added convenience of digital transfer.

Stimulus for Financial Innovation

One of the most promising applications of Bitcoin is as a platform for financial innovation. The Bitcoin protocol contains the digital blueprints for a number of useful financial and legal services that programmers can easily develop. Since bitcoins are, at their core, simply packets of data, they can be used to transfer, not only currencies, but also stocks, bets, and sensitive information.[55] Some of the features that are built into the Bitcoin protocol include micropayments, dispute mediations, assurance contracts, and smart property.[56] These features would allow for the easy development of Internet translation services, instantaneous processing for small transactions (like automatically metering Wi-Fi access), and Kickstarter-like crowdfunding services. Indeed, early initiatives have already materialized. The crowdfunding platform Pozible now allows project creators to amass microdonations in Bitcoin for minuscule transaction fees.[57] The payment platform Bitmonet provides internet content creators with a way to monetize their blog or portfolio with bitcoins.[58] Similarly, Beatcoin is a music delivery service powered through Bitcoin micropayments.[59] As the Bitcoin economy further matures, more of these innovative applications will continue to materialize.

Additionally, programmers can develop alternative protocols on top of the Bitcoin protocol in the same way that the Web and email are run on top of the Internet's TCP/IP protocol. One programmer has already proposed a new protocol layer to add on top of the Bitcoin protocol that can improve the network's stability and security.[60] Another programmer created a digital notary service to anonymously and securely store a "proof of existence" for private documents on top of the Bitcoin protocol.[61] Other programmers have adopted the Bitcoin model as a way to encrypt email communications.[62] Another group of developers has outlined an add-on protocol that will improve the privacy of the network.[63] Bitcoin is thus the foundation upon which other layers of functionality can be built. The Bitcoin project can be best thought of as a process of financial and communicative experimentation. Policymakers should take care that their directives do not quash the promising innovations developing within and on top of this fledgling protocol.

Challenges

Despite the benefits that it presents, Bitcoin has some downsides for potential users to consider. It has exhibited considerable price volatility throughout its existence. New users are at risk of improperly securing or even accidentally deleting their bitcoins if they are not cautious. Additionally, there are concerns about whether hacking could compromise the bitcoin economy.

Volatility

Bitcoin has weathered at least five significant price adjustments since 2011.[64] These adjustments resemble traditional speculative bubbles: overoptimistic media coverage of Bitcoin prompts waves of novice investors to pump up Bitcoin prices.[65] The exuberance reaches a tipping point, and the value eventually plummets. Newcomer investors eager to participate run the risk of overvaluing the currency and losing their money in a crash. Bitcoin's fluctuating value makes many observers skeptical of the currency's future.

Does this volatility foretell the end of Bitcoin? Some commentators believe so.[66] Others suggest that these fluctuations are stress-testing the currency and might eventually decrease in frequency as mechanisms develop to counteract volatility.[67] If bitcoins were only used as stores of value or units of account, the currency's volatility could indeed endanger its future. It does not make sense to manage business finances or keep savings in bitcoins if the market price swings wildly and unpredictably. When Bitcoin is used as a medium of exchange, however, volatility is less of a problem.[68] Merchants can price their wares in terms of a traditional currency and accept the equivalent number of bitcoins. Customers who purchase bitcoins to make a one-time purchase don't care about what the exchange rate will look like tomorrow; they simply care that Bitcoin can lower transaction costs in the present. Bitcoin's usefulness as a medium of exchange might explain why the currency has grown more popular among merchants in spite of its price volatility.[69] It is also possible that the value of bitcoins will become less volatile as more people become familiar with the Bitcoin technology and develop realistic expectations about its future.

Security Breaches

As a digital currency, Bitcoin presents some specific security challenges.[70] If people are not careful, they can inadvertently delete or misplace their bitcoins. Once the digital file is lost, the money is lost, just as with paper cash. If people do not protect their private Bitcoin addresses, they can leave themselves open to theft. Bitcoin wallets can now be protected by encryption, but users must choose to activate the encryption. If a user does not encrypt his or her wallet, bitcoins could be stolen through malware.[71] Bitcoin exchanges, too, have at times struggled with security; hackers successfully stole 24,000 BTC ($250,000) from a bitcoin exchange called Bitfloor in 2012[72] and mounted a massive series of distributed denial-of-service (DDoS) attacks against the most popular bitcoin exchange, Mt.Gox, in 2013.[73] (Bitfloor eventually repaid the stolen funds to its customers, and Mt.Gox ultimately recovered from the DDoS attacks.) More recently, the wallet and mixing service inputs.io lost an equivalent of $1.2 million of their customers' bitcoins to a hacking attack.[74] Unscrupulous exchange stewards have similarly been a problem; in November of 2013, GBL, a Chinese Bitcoin exchange, abruptly closed its website and absconded with $4.1 million worth of their customers' bitcoins.[75] While the accountable operator of inputs.io will compensate his customers with a partial refund, GBL customers are not so lucky. Combined with the GBL operators' duplicity, Bitcoin's irreversibility eradicates the possibility of recourse. Of course, many of the security risks facing Bitcoin are similar to those facing traditional currencies. Dollar bills can be destroyed or lost, personal financial information can be stolen and used by criminals, and banks can be robbed or targeted by DDoS attacks. Bitcoin users should take care to learn about and prepare for security concerns just as they currently do for other financial activities.

Criminal Uses

There are also reasons for policymakers to be apprehensive about some of Bitcoin's exaptations. Because Bitcoin is pseudonymous, policymakers and journalists have questioned whether criminals can use it to launder money and accept payment for illicit goods and services. Indeed, like cash, it can be used for ill as well as for good.

For one example, we can look at the shuttered Deep Web[76] black-market site known as "Silk Road." While in operation from February 2011 to October 2013, Silk Road took advantage of the anonymizing network Tor and the pseudonymous nature of Bitcoin to make available a vast digital marketplace where one could mail-order drugs and other licit and illicit wares. Although Silk Road administrators did not allow the exchange of any goods that resulted from fraud or harm, like stolen credit card information or photographs of child exploitation, it did allow merchants to sell illegal products like forged identity documents and illicit drugs. The pseudonymous nature of Bitcoin allowed buyers to purchase illegal goods online in the same way that cash has been traditionally used to facilitate illicit purchases in person. One study estimated the total monthly Silk Road transactions amounted to approximately $1.2 million.[77] But the Bitcoin market amassed $770 million in transactions during June 2013; Silk Road sales constituted a small drop in the total bitcoin economy bucket.[78]

Bitcoin's association with Silk Road has tarnished its reputation. Following the publication of an article on Silk Road in 2011,[79] senators Charles Schumer and Joe Manchin sent a letter to Attorney General Eric Holder and the Drug Enforcement Administration's administrator Michele Leonhart calling for a crackdown on Silk Road, the anonymizing software Tor, and Bitcoin.[80] Their concerns were quickly addressed. Following a two year investigation into the Deep Web market, the FBI shut down the Silk Road website on October 2, 2013 and arrested Ross Ulbricht, the man alleged to be its infamous operator known only as the "Dread Pirate Roberts."[81] The FBI confiscated all bitcoins associated with Silk Road, totaling an unprecedented seizure of 26,000 BTC, worth $3.6 million at the time of the transfer.[82] Many of the largest merchants on Silk Road, too, have been indicted since Silk Road's closure.[83] Still, the end of Silk Road has not eliminated the problem of illicit trade. Other Deep Web black markets, like Black Market Reloaded,[84]

Sheep Marketplace,[85] and the relaunched Silk Road 2.0,[86] present new challenges for law enforcement.

Another concern is that Bitcoin can be used to launder money for financing terrorism and trafficking in illegal goods. Although these worries are currently more theoretical than evidential, Bitcoin could indeed be an option for those who wish to discreetly move ill-gotten money. Concerns about Bitcoin's potential to facilitate money laundering were stoked after Liberty Reserve, a private, centralized digital-currency service based in Costa Rica, was shut down by authorities on charges of money laundering.[87]

While Liberty Reserve and Bitcoin appear similar because they both provide digital currencies, there are important differences between the two. Liberty Reserve was a centralized currency service created and owned by a private company, allegedly for the express purpose of facilitating money laundering. Bitcoin is not. The transactions within the Liberty Reserve economy were not transparent. Indeed, Liberty Reserve promised its customers anonymity. Bitcoin, on the other hand, is a decentralized open currency that provides a public record of all transactions. Money launderers may attempt to protect their Bitcoin addresses and identities, but their transaction records will always be public and accessible at any time by law enforcement. Laundering money through Bitcoin, then, can be seen as a much riskier undertaking than using a centralized system like Liberty Reserve. Additionally, several bitcoin exchanges have taken steps to comply with anti–money laundering record-keeping and reporting requirements.[88] The combination of a public ledger system and the cooperation of bitcoin exchanges in collecting information on their customers will likely make Bitcoin less attractive to launderers relative to private anonymous virtual currencies.

It is also important to note that many of the potential downsides of Bitcoin are the same as those facing traditional cash. Cash has historically been the vehicle of choice for drug traffickers and money launderers, but policymakers would never seriously consider banning cash. As regulators begin to contemplate Bitcoin, they should be wary of the perils of overregulation. In the worst-case scenario, regulators could prevent legitimate businesses from benefitting from the Bitcoin network without preventing money launderers and drug traffickers from using bitcoins. If bitcoin exchanges are overburdened by regulation and shut down, for instance, money launderers and drug traffickers could still put money into the network by paying a person in cash to transfer his or her bitcoins into their virtual wallets. In this scenario, beneficial transactions are prevented by overregulation while the targeted activities are still able to occur. The challenge for policymakers and regulators is how to develop a system of oversight that assuages their twin concerns about money laundering and illicit purchases without smothering the benefits that Bitcoin is poised to provide to legitimate users in their everyday lives.

Regulation

Current law and regulation does not envision a technology like Bitcoin, so it exists in something of a legal gray area. This is largely the case because Bitcoin does not exactly fit existing statutory definitions of currency or other financial instruments or institutions, making it difficult to know which laws apply and how.

This situation is reminiscent of regulatory uncertainty surrounding other new technologies, such as Voice over Internet Protocol (VoIP).[89] When VoIP first emerged, the Communications Act and Federal Communications Commission (FCC) regulations only contemplated voice communications over the traditional public switched telephone network. Like Bitcoin, VoIP competed with a highly regulated legacy network, was less expensive, and was often peer-topeer. To this day Congress and the FCC continue to grapple with VoIP policy questions, including which public-interest obligations should be required of VoIP providers and whether VoIP providers must comply with law-enforcement wiretap requests.

Luckily, however, Congress and the FCC have charted a path for VoIP that has clarified much of the regulatory ambiguity without saddling the new technology with the legacy regulatory burden intended for monopoly telephone service. As a result, VoIP has flourished as a technology, has introduced competition to a previously stagnant market, and has lowered costs and improved access for consumers. Policymakers should seek to achieve the same with Bitcoin.

Bitcoin has the properties of an electronic payments system, a currency, and a commodity, among other things. As a result, it will likely receive scrutiny from several regulators. Below is an outline of some of the questions confronting these agencies as they prepare to regulate Bitcoin.

Is Private Currency Legal?

One of the most common initial questions about Bitcoin is whether the online currency is legal, given the federal government's monopoly on issuing legal tender. The answer seems to be yes. The Constitution only prohibits the states from coining money.[90] Privately issued currencies are not forbidden, and in fact many local currencies are in circulation.[91] To promote local economies, businesspeople and lawmakers have developed several alternative currencies in recent years, such as the Cascadia Hour Exchange in Portland and Life Dollars in Bellingham, Washington.[92]

What private parties may not do is issue currency that resembles US money.[93] One notorious case is that of Bernard von NotHaus, who was convicted in 2011 after printing and distributing a gold-backed currency called the "Liberty Dollar." His crime was not that he issued an alternative currency, but that it was similar in appearance to the US dollar and that von NotHaus attempted to spend his currency into circulation as dollars and encouraged others to do so as well.[94] In contrast, Bitcoin is in no danger of being confused with US currency.

Money-Transmission Laws

A business that transmits funds from one person to another is a money transmitter and in 48 states and the District of Columbia must obtain a license to operate.[95] Money transmitters are also subject to the Bank Secrecy Act (BSA) as implemented by regulations from FinCEN. Additionally, the USA PATRIOT Act made it a criminal offense to operate an unlicensed money-transmission business.[96]

The purpose of state licensing of money transmission has traditionally been consumer protection.[97] Because money transmitters (such as money-order issuers) are typically not FDIC-insured banks, consumers can be left holding the bag if a money transmitter does not forward the funds to the intended recipient. Licensing attempts to minimize this risk. Money-transmitter licensing in the States became widespread after the widely publicized defaults of several money-order companies in the 1980s.[98]

The BSA, on the other hand, is intended to prevent or detect money laundering and terrorist financing.[99] It requires money transmitters and other financial institutions to register with FinCEN, implement anti-money-laundering programs, keep records of their customers, and report suspicious transactions and other data.

Because it's not a company or legal entity, but instead a global peer-to-peer network, Bitcoin itself can't be said to be a money transmitter. The question then is, Do any of the actors in the Bitcoin ecosystem fit the statutory definitions of "money transmitter" that would subject them to state and federal regulation?

In March 2013, FinCEN issued guidance on the application of the BSA to virtual currencies, which include Bitcoin. The guidance defines three categories of persons potentially subject to its regulations as money transmitters:

> A *user* is a person that obtains virtual currency to purchase goods or services. An *exchanger* is a person engaged as a business in the exchange of virtual currency for real currency, funds, or other virtual currency. An *administrator* is a person engaged as a business in issuing (putting into circulation) a virtual currency, and who has the authority to redeem (to withdraw from circulation) such virtual currency.[100]

We can apply each of these definitions to persons in the Bitcoin ecosystem. The clearest definition is that of an *exchanger*. If one is in the business of exchanging dollars for bitcoins or vice versa, then we can conclude that one is a money transmitter under this guidance and must register with FinCEN and comply with the relevant record-keeping and reporting requirements. Also, because states often look to FinCEN's determinations about which types of entities are or are not money transmitters, an exchanger likely must obtain state money-transmitter licenses as well.

Less straightforward are the obligations of mere "users" of Bitcoin. The guidance states that if one obtains bitcoins "to purchase real or virtual goods or services," then one is not a money transmitter and not subject to FinCEN's regulations. It does not explain, however, how the law applies if one obtains bitcoins *not* to purchase goods or services. Some other reasons why one might obtain bitcoins include (1) speculation that the price of bitcoins will go up, (2) simply because one trusts a virtual currency's stability more than that of a particular "real currency" (think of Argentina or Zimbabwe), or (3) because one wants to make a remittance to a family member overseas. In none of these cases would Bitcoin users be assured that they are exempted from FinCEN's registration, record-keeping, and reporting requirements. This creates an uncertain regulatory environment that might unduly dampen use of Bitcoin.

Most confusing is how the guidance applies to Bitcoin miners, who create new bitcoins by lending their computing power to the Bitcoin network. The third class of persons that it defines is "administrators," but the definition only applies to centralized virtual currencies in which a central authority creates the currency. For example, Amazon.com is clearly the administrator of its new "Amazon Coins" virtual currency.[101] The guidance, therefore, has a section addressing decentralized virtual currencies such as Bitcoin. According to that section, a miner who mines bitcoins and then uses them "to purchase real or virtual goods and services" is considered a user not subject to the regulations.[102] But if the miner sells the mined bitcoins "to another person for real currency or its equivalent" then the miner qualifies as a money transmitter subject to regulation.[103]

It is not clear how such regulation of miners as money transmitters would further either consumer protection or anti-money-laundering interests. Miners are not transmitting bitcoins from one party to another; they are creating new bitcoins from thin air. If miners sell the bitcoins they mine, there are only two parties to the transaction. As a result, there is neither a consumer to protect nor a potential criminal seeking to convert "dirty money" into clean money.

Finally, the guidance notes that FinCEN regulations define currency as the currency of a state, and so the guidance also refers to this definition as "real currency."[104] It then develops a new concept that it calls "virtual currency" on which all the guidance is predicated.[105] The guidance defines virtual currency as "a medium of exchange that operates like a currency in some environments, but does not have all the attributes of real currency."[106] It goes on to introduce another concept by stating that there are different kinds of "virtual currency" and that the present guidance only extends to "convertible virtual currency," which it defines as one that "either has an equivalent value in real currency, or acts as a substitute for real currency."[107] While the definition of currency (aka "real currency") was adopted through rulemaking, the other new and substantive concepts of "virtual currency" and "convertible virtual currency" exist only in the guidance. As a result, the guidance may be seen as encompassing new law and not merely interpretations of existing law or regulations, thus necessitating a rulemaking under the Administrative Procedure Act.

CFTC Regulation

By their nature, bitcoins can be conceived of either as a commodity or as a currency. Indeed, economist George Selgin has called Bitcoin "synthetic-commodity money."[108] This has attracted the attention of the Commodity Futures Trading Commission (CFTC), which has authority to regulate commodity futures and the markets in which they trade, as well as to regulate some foreign-exchange instruments.[109]

Bart Chilton, one of five CFTC commissioners, recently told the *Financial Times* that Bitcoin "is for sure something we need to explore."[110] Other sources confirmed that the CFTC is "seriously" looking at the virtual currency.[111] To the extent it chooses to regulate bitcoin transactions, one obvious question is whether CFTC will do so under its commodity futures or foreign-exchange authority.

While the Commodity Exchange Act defines “foreign-exchange forwards” and “foreign-exchange swaps,” it does not define “foreign exchange” or “foreign currency,” presumably because Congress considered the meaning of those terms obvious. Therefore, if the CFTC moves to apply its foreign-exchange regulations to Bitcoin transactions, it will have to make the determination that bitcoins are considered “foreign currency.” While conceivable, such a determination would be at odds with the common understanding of foreign currency, as the money coined by foreign governments.

To illustrate this, we can look at the 2009 Dodd-Frank Wall Street Reform and Consumer Protection Act, which expands the CFTC’s authority to regulate foreign exchange. Title 10 of the act also establishes the Consumer Financial Protection Bureau (CFPB), and for purposes of that title defines “foreign exchange” as “the exchange, for compensation, of currency of the United States or of a foreign government for currency of another government.”[112] This definition gives a hint of what Congress’s conception of “foreign exchange” is, and bitcoin exchange would clearly fall outside it, because bitcoins are not the currency of any government.

The connection between foreign currency and government issuance is commonplace. For example, the Treasury Department’s definition of currency (adopted through rulemaking, as noted earlier) is

> the coin and paper money of the United States or of any other country that is designated as legal tender and that circulates and is customarily used and accepted as a medium of exchange in the country of issuance. Currency includes US silver certificates, US notes and Federal Reserve notes. Currency also includes official foreign bank notes that are customarily used and accepted as a medium of exchange in a foreign country.[113]

This comports with the Uniform Commercial Code’s definition of “money,” which is “a medium of exchange authorized or adopted by a domestic or foreign government [including] a monetary unit of account established by an intergovernmental organization or by agreement between two or more nations.”[114]

In contrast, the CFTC would have no problem treating bitcoins as commodities. The Commodity Exchange Act defines commodities as all “goods and articles . . . and all services, rights, and interests . . . in which contracts for future delivery are presently or in the future dealt in," except onions and motion-picture box-office receipts.[115] Therefore, bitcoins could certainly qualify as a commodity because they are articles that can be traded and made subject to futures contracts. That said, it is interesting to note that bitcoins are unlike traditional commodities such as gold, corn, or oil, which are tangible and have intrinsically valuable uses. It is also important to note that the CFTC's authority is over, not commodities themselves, but commodity futures. An exchange of bitcoins for dollars or other national currency, however, typically occurs instantaneously, and not as part of a futures contract. Therefore, CFTC regulation of bitcoins *as commodities* may be limited. To the extent bitcoin futures markets develop, however, they will certainly be subject to CFTC supervision.[116]

Electronic Fund Transfer Regulation

The final possible vector for regulation of Bitcoin under existing law that we will consider is regulation under the Electronic Fund Transfer Act (EFTA)[117] and its application through the Federal Reserve's Regulation E.[118] The purpose of the EFTA is to establish the respective rights and responsibilities of consumers and financial institutions in electronic fund transfers.[119] Like the other laws and regulations we have seen, the EFTA does not seem to contemplate a decentralized virtual currency like Bitcoin.

The act defines electronic fund transfers as "any transfer of funds, other than a transaction originated by check, draft, or similar paper instrument, which is initiated through an electronic terminal, telephonic instrument, or computer or magnetic tape so as to order, instruct, or authorize a financial institution to debit or credit an account."[120] It further defines "financial institution" as "a State or National bank, a State or Federal savings and loan association, a mutual savings bank, a State or Federal credit union, or any other person who, directly or indirectly, holds an account belonging to a consumer."[121] These definitions, and the regulations they undergird, assume that electronic fund transfers will necessarily involve "financial institutions" and "accounts." Bitcoin, however, runs counter to that notion.

The Bitcoin system itself does not qualify as a "financial institution" because, as noted earlier, it is not a company or legal entity but instead a global peer-to-peer network. As a result, a Bitcoin address with which bitcoins are associated on the network cannot be said to be an account of a financial institution. Furthermore, as noted above in the technical discussion of how bitcoins are transferred between addresses, in the Bitcoin system there is no "financial institution" or other third party of any kind that "debit[s] or credit[s] an account." Electronic fund transfers between addresses are carried out by users alone, who sign a transaction with the private key associated with a Bitcoin address under their control. The Bitcoin network merely confirms that the transaction is legitimate.

While many users keep the "wallet files"[122] containing their private keys on their own computers or other devices,[123] some delegate securing their keys to online wallet services.[124] Such third-party wallet services often also provide greater ease-of-use than desktop Bitcoin software. Users typically create an "account" on such a wallet service, and their Bitcoin addresses are associated with those accounts. It is conceivable that such online services could fit the definition of "financial institution" under the EFTA, and thus be subject to the regulation. An argument could be made, however, that these services are not engaged in electronic fund transfers because they do not initiate transfers.[125] Transfers are made by the users directly and are verified by the Bitcoin network; online wallet services merely provide the software and storage that allows users to interact with the Bitcoin network.

Finally, new rules from the Consumer Financial Protection Bureau (CFPB) amending Regulation E target remittance-transfer providers. The regulations require remittance providers to disclose exchange rates and fees associated with international transfers, and to investigate and remediate processing errors.[126] They also require that consumers be afforded 30 minutes or more to cancel a transfer.[127] This requirement can be seen as incompatible with the Bitcoin protocol, because all bitcoin transactions are irreversible. One way to comply with this regulation might be to delay the execution of transactions. The real problem, though, is that this requirement is fundamentally at odds with the purpose of the technology.

Policy Recommendations

As we have seen, Bitcoin does not easily fit into existing regulatory boxes. That is often the hallmark of a disruptive technology. Indeed Bitcoin is a revolutionary technical achievement that heralds amazing potential benefits to human welfare. However, like any technology that can be used for good, it can also be used for ill. The challenge for policymakers will be to foster Bitcoin's beneficial uses while minimizing its negative consequences. We conclude with some recommendations to help policymakers meet this challenge.

Don't Restrict Bitcoin

Because Bitcoin is essentially online cash, some who trade in drugs and other illicit goods online have found it to be an ideal medium of exchange.[128] Confronted with this fact, the initial impulse of some policymakers will be to call for restrictions on the technology.[129] There are many good reasons, however, to resist such an impulse.

First, as a technology, Bitcoin is neither good nor bad; it is neutral. Paper dollar bills, like bitcoins, can be used in illicit transactions, yet we do not consider outlawing paper bills. We only prohibit their *illicit use*. Furthermore, there is only anecdotal evidence about the extent to which bitcoins are utilized in criminal transactions. It would be wise to put the criminal use of the technology in perspective alongside its legitimate uses. As the bitcoin economy grows, legitimate uses of bitcoins will likely dwarf criminal transactions,[130] just as we see with paper dollar bills.

Second, any attempt to restrict Bitcoin technology will only harm legitimate uses while leaving illicit uses largely unaffected. Because it is a decentralized global network, Bitcoin is virtually impossible to shut down. There is no Bitcoin company or other entity that can be targeted. Instead, Bitcoin and its ledger exist only in the distributed peer-to-peer network created by its users. As with the peer-to-peer file-sharing service BitTorrent, taking down any of the individual computers that make up the peer-to-peer system would have little effect on the rest of the network. Therefore, making the use of Bitcoin illegal would not undermine the network; it would only serve to ensure that law-abiding users are denied access to the technology. As a result, society would forgo enjoying the many potential benefits of Bitcoin without seeing any drop in criminal use.

Third, if Bitcoin were prohibited, the government would forego the opportunity to regulate intermediaries in the bitcoin economy, such as exchangers and money transmitters. The governmental interests in detecting and preventing money laundering and terrorist financing would be better advanced, not by prohibiting the technology, but by requiring intermediaries to keep records and report suspicious activities, just as traditional financial institutions do. Again, restricting the use of Bitcoin will only ensure that criminals alone will use the technology. Any illicit intermediaries that emerge, such as exchanges and payment processors, will be unregulated.

Finally, even if the United States prohibited the use of Bitcoin, it is likely that many other countries would not, recognizing the technology's many potential benefits. The Finnish central bank, for example, has stated that the digital currency is not illegal,[131] and as a result many Finnish businesses have begun to accept bitcoins.[132] By prohibiting Bitcoin use, the United States could put itself at an international competitive disadvantage in the development and use of what may be the next-generation payments system.

Normalize Regulation and Encourage Further Development

Rather than overreact to illicit uses of Bitcoin, policymakers would be wise to take a calm and careful approach to the challenges posed by the new technology. Doing so would allow law enforcement to pursue its interests in detecting and preventing money laundering and terrorist financing while ensuring that society does not forgo Bitcoin's many benefits. Luckily, regulators to date have taken such a cautious approach by slowly integrating Bitcoin into the existing financial regulatory framework. Policymakers can take a few basic steps to maintain the right balance.

In the short term, FinCEN should clarify its recent guidance, especially as it relates to miners and users who do not obtain bitcoins to purchase goods or services, but instead do so for other legal and legitimate purposes. It should do this by welcoming public participation of the Bitcoin community of developers, miners, businesses, and users in formal public notice and comment proceedings. While FinCEN's mission is to safeguard the financial system from illicit use, it also has an obligation not to unduly hinder its technological development. Working with Bitcoin's legitimate users, there is no doubt FinCEN can achieve its goals while minimizing regulatory uncertainty.

In the long term, policymakers should better define Bitcoin's broader regulatory status. As we have seen, the digital currency does not comfortably fit any existing classification or legal definition. It is not a foreign currency, nor a traditional commodity, nor is it simply a payments network. Consequently, applying existing rules to Bitcoin could unduly impede Bitcoin's legitimate development without any attendant gains to law enforcement or consumer welfare. As a result, policymakers may want to consider developing a new category that takes into account the technology's unique nature. They should also carefully consider what regulation, if any, bitcoin exchanges, payment processors, and users should face.

Finally, policymakers should not only allow Bitcoin's development to continue unimpeded, they should help foster its growth by revisiting existing regulatory barriers. One of the greatest obstacles to Bitcoin's legitimate adoption is the requirement that businesses engaging in money transmission acquire a license from each state. This is a duplicative, laborious, and expensive process that presents a barrier to interstate commerce without much benefit to consumers. Federal lawmakers and regulators should consider whether preemption is necessary.

CONCLUSION

Bitcoin is an exciting innovation that has the potential to greatly improve human welfare and jump-start beneficial and potentially revolutionary developments in payments, communications, and business. Bitcoin's clever use of public-key encryption and peer-to-peer networking solves the double-spending problem that had previously made decentralized digital currencies impossible. These properties combine to create a payment system that could lower transactions costs in business and remittances, alleviate poverty, provide an escape from capital controls and monetary mismanagement, allow for legitimate financial privacy online, and spur new financial innovations. On the other hand, as "digital cash," Bitcoin can be used for money laundering and illicit trade. Banning Bitcoin is not the solution to ending money laundering and illicit trade, just as banning cash is not a solution to these same ills.

Bitcoin could ultimately fail as an experimental digital currency and payment system. An unanticipated problem could arise and undermine the bitcoin economy. A superior cryptocurrency could outcompete and replace Bitcoin. It could simply fizzle out as a fad. The possibilities for failure are endless, but one reason for failure should not be that policymakers did not understand its workings and potential. We are ultimately advocating not for Bitcoin, but for innovation. It is important that policymakers allow this experimentation to continue. Policymakers should work to clarify how Bitcoin is regulated and to normalize its regulation so that we have the opportunity to learn just how innovative Bitcoin can be.

End Notes

[1] The attached appendix is an updated version of *Bitcoin: A Primer for Policymakers* by me and Andrea Castillo, which goes into considerable detail about the technical workings of Bitcoin, as well as a detailed description of the cryptocurrency's potential benefits not just for consumers and the economy, but also for free speech and oppressed minorities around the world. It also looks at Bitcoin's challenges, including the currency's security and volatility, as well as law enforcement concerns and regulatory alternatives.

[2] The FBI has reported that total revenues generated by Silk Road were 9,519,664 bitcoins. Criminal Complaint against Ross Ulbricht, page 15, available at http://www1.icsi.berkeley.

edu/~nweaver/UlbrichtCriminalComplaint.pdf. That has been erroneously reported as the equivalent of over $1 billion in sales. Id. The error lies in simply multiplying the number of bitcoins by the exchange rate at the time of Ulbricht's arrest. This does not take into account the fact that bitcoins fluctuated in value widely from the time of Silk Road's inception to the present, so that the actual sales figure in dollars is much less than $1 billion. Nicolas Christin of Carnegie Mellon University has conducted the most rigorous estimates of Silk Road's revenues prior to its seizure. Nicolas Christin, "Traveling the Silk Road: A Measurement Analysis of a Large Anonymous Online Marketplace,' Carnegie Mellon CyLab Technical Reports: CMU-CyLab-12-018, July 30, 2012 (updated November 28, 2012), http://www.cylab.cmu .edu/files/pdfs/tech_reports/CMUCyLab12018.pdf. In forthcoming work he estimates that over its life Silk Road actually generated revenues of between $100 and $200 million.

[3] *U.S. v. Liberty Reserve, et al.* Indictment at 9 & 12, http://www.justice.gov/usao/nys /pressreleases/May13 /LibertyReserveetalDocuments/Liberty%20Reserve,%20et%20al.% 20Indictment%20-%20Redacted.pdf.

[4] China has emerged as the fastest growing market for Bitcoin, with 33 percent of the world's bitcoins now flowing through a Chinese Bitcoin exchange, BTC China. Robert McMillan, "This Chinese Exchange Just Pushed the Value of Bitcoins over $200,' *WIRED*, October 23, 2013, http://www.wired.com/wiredenterprise/2013/10/btc-china/. Canada has pursued a progressive approach toward Bitcoin with FINTRAC, that country's equivalent of FinCEN, determining that exchanges and other businesses need not register as money transmitters. Jeremy Kirk, "Canadian Regulator Takes Lighter View of Bitcoin," *PC World*, May 21, 2013, http://www.pcworld.com/article/2039347/canadian-regulator -takes-lighter-view-of-bitcoin.html. As a result, Vancouver (and not San Francisco or New York) boasts the world's first bitcoin ATM. Vivian Luk, "First Ever Bitcoin ATM Goes Live in Vancouver, but Experts Warn of Risks," *Vancouver Sun*, October 30, 2013, http://www.vancouversun.com/business/your-money/First+ever+Bitcoin+goes+live+ Vancouver+experts+warn/9099351/story.html.

[5] For example, FinCEN issued its March guidance without providing any notice or providing the public an opportunity to comment. While that guidance clarified Bitcoin's regulatory treatment, it also introduced regulatory uncertainty around several specific use cases that would have no doubt been easily spotted by the Bitcoin community had it been given the opportunity. See *infra* 19–21. Since then FinCEN has begun to better engage with the Bitcoin community.

End Notes for Appendix

[1] Jerry Brito is a senior research fellow at the Mercatus Center at George Mason University.

[2] Andrea Castillo is a research assistant at the Mercatus Center at George Mason University.

[3] Financial information provided at bitcoincharts.com estimates total market capitalization to be $4,097,390,850 as of November 12, 2013.

[4] Sarah E. Needleman and Spencer E. Ante, "Bitcoin Startups Begin to Attract Real Cash," *Wall Street Journal*, May 8, 2013, http://online.wsj.com/article/SB1000142412788 732368760 4578469012375269952.html.

[5] François R. Velde, "Bitcoin: A Primer," *Essays On Issues*, Number 317, Federal Reserve Bank of Chicago, December 2013, http://www.chicagofed.org/digital_assets/publications /chicago_fed_letter/2013 /cfldecember2013_317.pdf.

[6] US Department of the Treasury, Financial Crimes and Enforcement Network, "Application of FinCEN's Regulations to Persons Administering, Exchanging, or Using Virtual Currencies" (Regulatory Guidance, FIN-2013- G001, US Department of the Treasury, Washington, DC, March 18, 2013), http://fincen.gov/statutes_regs/guidance /html/FIN-2013-G001.html.

[7] Jennifer Shasky Calvery, "Combating Transnational Organized Crime: International Money Laundering as a Threat to Our Financial Systems" (Statement for the Record Before the Subcommittee on Crime, Terrorism, and Homeland Security of the House Committee on the Judiciary, February 8, 2012), http://www.justice.gov/ola /testimony/112-2/02-08-12-crm-shasky-calvery-testimony.pdf.

[8] US Government Accountability Office, "Virtual Economies and Currencies: Additional IRS Guidance Could Reduce Compliance Risks" (report to the Senate Committee on Finance, GAO-13-516, May, 2013), http://www .gao.gov/assets/660/654620.pdf.

[9] Tracy Alloway, Gregory Meyer, and Stephen Foley, "US Regulators Eye Bitcoin Supervision," *Financial Times*, May 6, 2013, http://www.ft.com/intl/cms/s/0/b810157c-b651-11e2-93ba-00144feabdc0.html.

[10] David Chaum, "Achieving Electronic Privacy," *Scientific American*, August 1992, 96–101.

[11] "Markets," Bitcoincharts, accessed July 30, 2013, http://bitcoincharts.com/markets/.

[12] Christof Paar, Jan Pelzl, and Bart Preneel, "Introduction to Public-Key Cryptography," chapter 6 in *Understanding Cryptography: A Textbook for Students and Practitioners*, ed. Christof Paar and Jan Pelzl (New York: Springer, 2010). Sample available at http://wiki.crypto.rub.de/Buch/download/Understanding-Cryptography -Chapter6.pdf.

[13] Miners tend to be ordinary computer enthusiasts, but as mining becomes more difficult and expensive, the activity will likely become somewhat professionalized. For more information, see Alec Liu, "A Guide to Bitcoin Mining," *Motherboard*, March 22, 2013, http://motherboard.vice.com/blog/a-guide-to-bitcoin-mining-why-someone-bought -a-1500-bitcoin-miner-on-ebay-for-20600.

[14] Ken Tindell, "Geeks Love the Bitcoin Phenomenon Like They Loved the Internet in 1995," *Business Insider*, April 5, 2013, http://www.businessinsider.com/how-bitcoins-are-mined-and-used-2013-4.

[15] Note that this might be a boon to economic researchers.

[16] *Bitcoin wiki*, s.v. "Address," accessed July 30, 2013, https://en.bitcoin.it/wiki/Address.

[17] Elli Androulaki et al., "Evaluating User Privacy in Bitcoin," *IACR Cryptology ePrint Archive* 596 (2012), http://fc13.ifca.ai/proc/1-3.pdf.

[18] Fergal Reid and Martin Harrigan, "An Analysis of Anonymity in the Bitcoin System," in *Security and Privacy in Social Networks*, ed. Yaniv Altshuler et al. (New York: Springer, 2013), http://arxiv.org/pdf/1107.4524v2.pdf.

[19] Dorit Ron and Adi Shamir, "Quantitative Analysis of the Full Bitcoin Transaction Graph," *IACR Cryptology ePrint Archive* 584 (2012), http://eprint.iacr.org/2012/584.pdf.

[20] Entity merging is the process of observing two or more public keys used as an input to one transaction at the same time. In this way, even if a user has several different public keys, an observer can gradually link them together and remove the ostensible anonymity that multiple public keys is thought to provide.

[21] Micha Ober, Stefan Katzenbeisser, and Kay Hamacher, "Structure and Anonymity of the Bitcoin Transaction Graph," *Future Internet* 5, no. 2 (2013), http://www.mdpi.com/1999-5903/5/2/237.

[22] Tom Simonite, "Bitcoin Hits the Big Time, to the Regret of Some Early Boosters," *MIT Technology Review*, May 22, 2013, http://www.technologyreview.com/news/515061 /bitcoin-hits-the-big-time-to-the-regret-of-some-early -boosters/.

[23] Gabrielle Karol, "Small Business Owners Say Bitcoins Better Than Credit Cards," *FOX Business, Small Business Center*, April 12, 2013, http://smallbusiness.foxbusiness.com /entrepreneurs/2013/04/12/small-business-owners-say -bitcoins-better-than-credit-cards/.

[24] Bailey Reutzel, "Why Some Merchants Accept Bitcoin Despite the Risks," *Payments Source*, May 21, 2013, http://www.paymentssource.com/news/why-some-merchants-accept-bitcoin-despite-the-risks-3014183-1.html.

[25] Bailey Reutzel, "Some Risky Merchants Turn to Bitcoin Processor; Others Go It Alone," *Payments Source*, November 8, 2013, http://www.paymentssource.com/news/some-risky-merchants-turn-to-bitcoin-processor-others -go-it-alone-3015974-1.html.

[26] Emily Maltby, "Chargebacks Create Business Headaches," *Wall Street Journal*, February 10, 2011, http://online.wsj.com/article/SB10001424052748704698004576104554234202010.html. One such scam involves Alice sending Bob a PayPal payment for a laptop that Bob has listed on Craigslist. Alice comes by Bob's house, picks up the laptop, and soon thereafter initiates a "charge-back" (i.e., reverses the payment). PayPal generally requires proof of shipment before reversing a charge-back, so Bob is out of luck.

[27] Rob Wile, "A Brooklyn Bodega Owner Told Us Why All Merchants Should Start Accepting Bitcoin," *Business Insider*, November 11, 2013, http://www.businessinsider.com/brooklyn-bitcoin-bodega-2013-11.

[28] Vitalik Buterin, "Bitcoin Store Opens: All Your Electronics Cheaper with Bitcoins," *Bitcoin Magazine*, November 5, 2012, http://bitcoinmagazine.com/bitcoin-store-opens-all-your-electronics-cheaper-with-bitcoins/.

[29] Amazon listing for a Samsung Galaxy Note tablet, accessed May 29, 2013, http://amzn.com/B00BJXNGIK.

[30] Bitcoin store listing for a Samsung Galaxy Note tablet, accessed May 29, 2013, https://www.bitcoinstore.com/samsung-galaxy-note-gt-n8013-10-1-32-gb-tablet-wi-fi-1-40-ghz-deep-gray.html. Products on the Bitcoin store are priced in both bitcoins and US dollars. At the point of purchase, Bitpay, a Bitcoin payment processing company, determines the currency conversion rate and holds that price for 15 minutes. See the Bitcoin Store FAQ: https://www.bitcoinstore.com/faq.

[31] World Bank Payment Systems Development Group, *Remittance Prices Worldwide: An Analysis of Trends in the Average Total Cost of Migrant Remittance Services* (Washington, DC: World Bank, 2013), http://remittanceprices.worldbank.org/~/media/FPDKM /Remittances/Documents/RemittancePriceWorldwide -Analysis-Mar2013.pdf.

[32] Ibid.

[33] Jessica Silver-Greenberg, "New Rules for Money Transfers, but Few Limits," *New York Times*, June 1, 2012, http://www.nytimes.com/2012/06/02/business/new-rules-for-money-transfers-but-few-limits.html?pagewanted =all&_r=0.

[34] World Bank, *Remittance Prices*.

[35] *Bitcoin wiki*, s.v. "Transaction fees," accessed July 30, 2013, https://en.bitcoin.it/wiki /Transaction_fees.

[36] Andrew Paul, "Is Bitcoin the Next Generation of Online Payments?," *Yahoo! Small Business Advisor*, May 24, 2013, http://smallbusiness.yahoo.com/advisor/bitcoin-next-generation-online-payments-213922448--finance.html.

[37] Simonite, "Bitcoin Hits the Big Time."

[38] Andrew R. Johnson, "Money Transfers in Bitcoins? Western Union, MoneyGram Weigh the Option," *Wall Street Journal*, April 18, 2013, http://online.wsj.com/article/SB10001424127887324493704578431000719258048.html.

[39] Muhammad Yunus, *Banker to the Poor: Micro-lending and the Battle against World Poverty* (New York: Public Affairs, 2003).

[40] Oya Pinar Ardic, Maximilien Heimann, and Nataliya Mylenko, "Access to Financial Services and the Financial Inclusion Agenda around the World" (Policy Research Working Paper, World Bank Financial and Private Sector Development Consultative Group to Assist the Poor, 2011), https://openknowledge.worldbank.org/bitstream/handle/10986/3310 /WPS 5537. pdf.

[41] Jeff Fong, "How Bitcoin Could Help the World's Poorest People," *PolicyMic*, May 2013, http://www.policymic .com/articles/41561/bitcoin-price-2013-how-bitcoin-could-help-the-world-s-poorest-people.

[42] Emily Spaven, "Kipochi launches M-Pesa Integrated Bitcoin Wallet in Africa," *CoinDesk*, July 19, 2013, http:// www.coindesk.com/kipochi-launches-m-pesa-integrated-bitcoin-wallet-in-africa/.

[43] "Bitcoin Statistics," LocalBitcoins.com, accessed November 12, 2013, https://localbitcoins.com/statistics.

[44] Bailey Ruetzel, "Buttercoin Takes a Different Path to Handling Virtual Currency," *Payments Source*, September 9, 2013, http://www.paymentssource.com/news/buttercoin-takes-a-different-path-to-handling-virtual-currency3015366-1.html.

[45] Kim-Mai Cutler, "YC-Backed Buttercoin Uses Bitcoin To Attack the $500B-A-Year Remittances Economy," *Techcrunch*, August 20, 2013, http://techcrunch.com/2013/08/20/buttercoin/.

[46] Vitalik Buterin, "Charity Focus: Sean's Outpost," *Bitcoin Magazine*, April 2013, http://bitcoinmagazine.com /sandbox/seansoutpost.pdf.

[47] Ibid.

[48] Vitalik Buterin, "Sean's Outpost Announces Satoshi Forest, Nine-Acre Sanctuary for the Homeless," *Bitcoin Magazine*, September 9, 2023, http://bitcoinmagazine.com/6939/seans-outpost-announces-satoshi-forest/.

[49] Meghan Lords, "Feeding and Housing the Homeless with Bitcoin," *Bitcoin Not Bombs*, August 16, 2013, http:// www.bitcoinnotbombs.com/feeding-and-housing-the-homeless-with-bitcoin/.

[50] Jon Matonis, "Bitcoin's Promise in Argentina," *Forbes*, April 27, 2013, http://www.forbes.com/sites/jonmatonis /2013/04/27/bitcoins-promise-in-argentina/.

[51] Roberto A. Ferdman, "Argentina's Unofficial Consumer Confidence Metric is Free-Falling Again," *Quartz*, October 23, 2013, http://qz.com/138498/argentinas-unofficial-consumer-confidence-metric-is-free-falling-again/.

[52] Camila Russo, "Bitcoin Dreams Endure to Savers Crushed by CPI: Argentina Credit," *Bloomberg*, April 16, 2013, http://www.bloomberg.com/news/2013-04-16/bitcoin-dreams-endure-to-savers-crushed-by-cpi-argentina-credit .html.

[53] Georgia Wells, "Bitcoin Downloads Surge in Argentina," *Wall Street Journal Money Beat*, July 17, 2013, http:// blogs.wsj.com/moneybeat/2013/07/17/bitcoin-downloads-surge-in-argentina/.

[54] Ben Smith and Conz Preti, "Argentina's Net Party Is Ready for the Revolution," *Buzzfeed*, October 24, 2013, http://www.buzzfeed.com/bensmith/argentinas-net-party-is-ready-for-the-revolution.

[55] Jerry Brito, "The Top 3 Things I Learned at the Bitcoin Conference," *Reason*, May 20, 2013, http://reason.com /archives/2013/05/20/the-top-3-things-i-learned-at-the-bitcoi.

[56] Mike Hearn, "Bitcoin 2012 London: Mike Hearn," YouTube video, 28:19, posted by "QueuePolitely," September 27, 2012, http://www.youtube.com/watch?v=mD 4L7x DNCmA. Smart property is a concept to control ownership of an item through agreements made in the Bitcoin block chain. Smart property allows people to exchange ownership of a good or service once a condition is met using cryptography. Although smart property is still theoretical, the basic mechanisms are built into the Bitcoin protocol. See *Bitcoin wiki*, s.v., "Smart Property," accessed July 30, 2013, https://en.bitcoin.it/wiki/Smart_Property.

[57] "Pozible Now Accepting Pledges in Bitcoin," *Pozible Blog*, October 2013, http://www.pozible.com/blog/article /index/129.

[58] John Biggs, "Bitmonet Monetizes Your Blog Through the Power of Bitcoin, " *Techcrunch*, August 30, 2013, http://considertechcrunch.com/2013/08/30/bitmonet-monetizes-your-blog-through-the-power-of-bitcoin/.

[59] Romain Dillet, "Beatcoin is a Music Jukebox Hack Powered By Bitcoin Micropayments," *Techcrunch*, October 27, 2013, http://techcrunch.com/2013/10/27/beatcoin-is-a-music-jukebox-hack-powered-by-bitcoin-micropayments/.

[60] J. R. Willett, "The Second Bitcoin Whitepaper" (white paper, 2013), https://sites.google.com /site fradicates the possibility forie hyphens up in here?emerging and another underlying class? If so, leave as is. If not, consider/2ndbtcwpaper/2ndBitcoinWhitepaper.pdf.

[61] Jeremy Kirk, "Could the Bitcoin Network Be Used as an Ultrasecure Notary Service?," *ComputerWorld*, May 23, 2013, http://www.computerworld.com/s/article/9239513/Could_the_Bitcoin_network_be_used_as_an_ultrasecure _notary_service_.

[62] Jonathan Warren, "Bitmessage: A Peer-to-Peer Message Authentication and Delivery System" (white paper, November 27, 2012), https://bitmessage.org/bitmessage.pdf.

[63] Ian Miers et al., "Zerocoin: Anonymous Distributed E-Cash from Bitcoin" (working paper, the Johns Hopkins University Department of Computer Science, Baltimore, MD, 2013), http://spar.isi.jhu.edu/~mgreen /ZerocoinOakland.pdf.

[64] Timothy B. Lee, "An Illustrated History of Bitcoin Crashes," *Forbes*, April 11, 2013, http://www.forbes.com/sites /timothylee/2013/04/11/an-illustrated-history-of-bitcoin-crashes/.

[65] Felix Salmon, "The Bitcoin Bubble and the Future of Currency," *Medium*, April 3, 2013, https://medium.com /money-banking/2b5ef79482cb.

[66] Maureen Farrell, "Strategist Predicts End of Bitcoin," *CNNMoney*, May 14, 2013, http://money.cnn.com/2013/05 /14/investing/bremmer-bitcoin/index.html.

[67] Adam Gurri, "Bitcoins, Free Banking, and the Optional Clause," *Ümlaut*, May 6, 2013, http://theumlaut.com/2013 /05/06/bitcoins-free-banking-and-the-optional-clause/.

[68] Jerry Brito, "Why Bitcoin's Valuation Really Doesn't Matter," *Technology Liberation Front*, April 5, 2013, http:// techliberation.com/2013/04/05/why-bitcoins-valuation-doesnt-really-matter/.

[69] Today, merchant service providers accept the risk presented by the volatility and nevertheless maintain low fees. It remains to be seen whether this model will be sustainable in the long run.

[70] Most of the security challenges concern wallet services and bitcoin exchanges. The protocol itself has proven to be considerably resilient to hacking and security risks. Renowned security researcher Dan Kaminsky tried, but failed, to hack the Bitcoin protocol in 2011. See Dan Kaminsky, "I Tried Hacking Bitcoin and I Failed," *Business Insider*, April 12, 2013, http://www.businessinsider.com/dan-kaminsky-highlights-flaws-bitcoin-2013-4.

[71] Stephen Doherty, "All Your Bitcoins Are Ours . . . ," *Symantec Blog*, June 16, 2011, http://www.symantec.com /connect/blogs/all-your-bitcoins-are-ours.

[72] Devin Coldewey, "$250,000 Worth of Bitcoins Stolen in Net Heist," *NBC News*, September 5, 2012, http://www .nbcnews.com/technology/250-000-worth-bitcoins-stolen-net-heist-980871.

[73] Meghan Kelly, "Fool Me Once: Bitcoin Exchange Mt.Gox Falls after Third DDoS Attack This Month," *VentureBeat*, April 21, 2013, http://venturebeat.com/2013/04/21/mt-gox-ddos/.

[74] Robert McMillan, "$1.2M Hack Shows Why You Should Never Store Bitcoins on the Internet," *Wired*, November 7, 2013, http://www.wired.com/wiredenterprise /2013/11 /inputs/.

[75] Jim Edwards, "A Bitcoin Exchange Holding $4.1 Million for 1,000 Customers Has Simply Vanished," *Business Insider*, November 12, 2013.

[76] *Wikipedia*, s.v. "Deep Web," accessed July 30, 2013, http://en.wikipedia.org/wiki/Deep_Web.

[77] Nicolas Christin, "Traveling the Silk Road: A Measurement Analysis of a Large Anonymous Online Marketplace," *Carnegie Mellon CyLab Technical Reports: CMU-CyLab-12-018*, July 30, 2012 (updated November 28, 2012), http://www.cylab.cmu.edu/files/pdfs /tech_reports/CMUCyLab12018.pdf.

[78] Jerry Brito, "*National Review* Gets Bitcoin Very Wrong," *Technology Liberation Front*, June 20, 2013, http:// techliberation.com/2013/06/20/national-review-gets-bitcoin-very-wrong/.

[79] Adrian Chen, "The Underground Website Where You Can Buy Any Drug Imaginable," *Gizmodo*, June 1, 2011, http://gawker.com/5805928/the-underground-website-where-you-can-buy-any-drug-imaginable.

[80] Brett Wolf, "Senators Seek Crackdown on 'Bitcoin' Currency," *Reuters*, June 8, 2011, http://www.reuters.com/article/2011/06/08/us-financial-bitcoins-idUSTRE7573T320 110608.

[81] Emily Flitter, "FBI Shuts Alleged online Drug Marketplace, Silk Road," *Reuters*, October 2, 2013, http://www .reuters.com/article/2013/10/02/us-crime-silkroad-raid-idUSBRE9910 TR20131002.

[82] James Ball, Charles Arthur, and Adam Gabbatt, "FBI Claims Largest Bitcoin Seizure After Arrest of Alleged Silk Road Founder," *The Guardian*, October 2, 2013, http://www.theguardian.com/technology/2013/oct/02/alleged-silk -road-website-founder-arrested-bitcoin.

[83] Brian Krebs, "Feds Arrest Alleged Top Silk Road Drug Dealer," *Krebs on Security*, October 7, 2013, http:// krebsonsecurity.com/2013/10/feds-arrest-alleged-top-silk-road-drug-seller/.

[84] Ryan Mac, "False Alarm: Silk Road Competitor Black Market Reloaded Staying Online," *Forbes*, October 18, 2013, http://www.forbes.com/sites/ryanmac/2013/10/18/false-alarm-silk-road-competitor-black-market-reloaded -staying-online/.

[85] Leonid Bershidsky, "Goodbye Silk Road, Hello Sheep Marketplace," *Bloomberg*, October 4, 2013, http://www .bloomberg.com/news/2013-10-04/goodbye-silk-road-hello-sheep-marketplace.html.

[86] Andy Greenberg, "'Silk Road 2.0' Launches, Promising A Resurrected Black Market for the Dark Web," *Forbes*, November 6, 2013, http://www.forbes.com/sites/andygreenberg /2013/11/06/silk-road-2-0-launches-promising-a -resurrected-black-market-for-the-dark-web/.

[87] "Liberty Reserve Digital Money Service Forced Offline," *BBC News—Technology*, May 27, 2013, http://www .bbc.co.uk/news/technology-22680297.

[88] Jeffrey Sparshott, "Bitcoin Exchange Makes Apparent Move to Play by U.S. Money-Laundering Rules," *Wall Street Journal*, June 28, 2013, http://online.wsj.com/article/SB 10001424127887323873904578574000957464468 .html.

[89] Sam Rozenfeld, "FCC'S VoIP Regulation Dilemma," *Telephony Your Way*, April 30, 2011, http://www .telephonyyourway.com/2011/04/30/fccs-voip-regulation-dilemma/.

[90] U.S. Const. art I § 10.

[91] Reuben Grinberg, "Bitcoin: An Innovative Alternative Digital Currency," *Hastings Science & Technology Law Journal* 4 (2011): 159–208.

[92] Blake Ellis, "Local Currencies: 'In the U.S. We Don't Trust,'" *CNN Money*, January 27, 2012, http://money.cnn .com/2012/01/17/pf/local_currency/index.htm.

[93] 18 U.S.C. §§ 485 and 486.

[94] Grinberg, "Bitcoin," 193n158.

[95] *Hearing on the Regulation of Non-bank Money Transmitter—Money Services Businesses*, 112th Congress (2012) (statement of Ezra C. Levine), testimony before the Subcommittee on Financial Institutions and Consumer Credit of the House Committee on Financial Services, http://financialservices.house.gov/uploadedfiles/hhrg-112-ba15-wstate -elevine-20120621.pdf.

[96] 18 U.S.C. § 1960.

[97] Aaron Greenspan, *Held Hostage: How the Banking Sector Has Distorted Financial Regulation and Destroyed Technological Progress* (Palo Alto, CA: Think Computer Corporation, 2011), http://www.thinkcomputer.com /corporate/whitepapers/heldhostage.pdf.

[98] Ibid., 3.

[99] 31 U.S.C. § 5311.

[100] FinCEN, *Application of FinCEN's Regulations*.

[101] Ingrid Lunden, "Amazon Now Offers Amazon Coins Virtual Currency on Kindle Fire, Gives $5 in Free Coins to All Users," *TechCrunch*, May 13, 2013, http://techcrunch.com/2013 /05/13/amazon-launches-amazon-coins-virtual -currency-on-kindle-fire-gives-5-in-free-coins-to-all-users/.

[102] Ibid.

[103] Ibid.

[104] FinCEN, *Application of FinCEN's Regulations*.

[105] Ibid.

[106] Ibid.

[107] Ibid.

[108] George Selgin, "Synthetic Commodity Money" (working paper, Department of Economics, University of Georgia, Athens, 2013), http://papers.ssrn.com/sol3/papers.cfm? abstract_ id=2000118.

[109] 7 U.S.C. §§ 2(C) and 2(E).

[110] Alloway, Meyer, and Foley, "US Regulators Eye Bitcoin."

[111] Ibid.

[112] Dodd-Frank Wall Street Reform and Consumer Protection Act § 1002 (16); 12 U.S.C. § 5481 (16) (2012).

[113] 31 C.F.R. § 1010.100(m).

[114] Unif. Commercial Code §§ 1–201.

[115] 7 U.S.C. § 1a (9).

[116] There are, however, emerging Bitcoin futures markets. See Cyrus Farivar, "'Taming the Bubble': Investors Bet on Bitcoin via Derivatives Markets," *Ars Technica*, April 11, 2013,

http://arstechnica.com/business/2013/04/taming -the-bubble-investors-bet-on-bitcoin-via-derivatives-markets/.

[117] 15 U.S.C. §§ 1601–1692 (2013).

[118] 12 C.F.R. §§ 205.1–205.20.

[119] 15 U.S.C. § 1693(b).

[120] 15 U.S.C. § 1693a (7).

[121] 15 U.S.C. § 1693a (9).

[122] *Bitcoin wiki*, s.v. "Wallet," accessed July 30, 2013, https://en.bitcoin.it/wiki/Wallet.

[123] Matthew Sparks, "Winklevoss Twins Back Bitcoin as Bubble Bursts," *Telegraph*, April 12, 2013, http://www.telegraph.co.uk/technology/news/9989610/Winklevoss-twins-back-bitcoin-as-bubble-bursts.html.

[124] *Bitcoin wiki*, "EWallet," accessed July 30, 2013, https://en.bitcoin.it/wiki/EWallet.

[125] Nikolei M. Kaplanov, "Nerdy Money: Bitcoin, the Private Digital Currency, and the Case against Its Regulation," *Loyola Consumer Law Review* 25, no. 1 (2012).

[126] Consumer Financial Protection Bureau, "Summary of the Final Remittance Transfer Rule (Amendment to Regulation E)" (Washington, DC: Consumer Financial Protection Bureau, 2013), http://files.consumerfinance.gov/f/201305_cfpb_remittance-transfer-rule_ summary.pdf.

[127] Ibid.

[128] Andy Greenberg, "Founder of Drug Site Silk Road Says Bitcoin Booms and Busts Won't Kill His Black Market," *Forbes*, April 16, 2013, http://www.forbes.com/sites /andygreenberg/2013/04/16/founder-of-drug-site-silk -road-says-bitcoin-booms-and-busts-wont-kill-his-black-market/.

[129] Charles Schumer and Joe Manchin, Letter to Attorney General Eric Holder and Drug Enforcement Administration Administrator Michele Leonhart, June 6, 2011. Available at http://www.manchin.senate.gov/public /index.cfm/press-releases?ID=284ae54a-acf1-4258-be1c-7acee1f7e8b3.

[130] Jan Jahosky, "BitPay Eclipses Silk Road in Bitcoin Sales with Explosive $5.2M March," *BitPay Blog*, April 2, 2013, http://blog.bitpay.com/2013/04/bitpay-eclipses-silk-road-in-bitcoin.html.

[131] Matt Clinch, "Bitcoin Utopia? Interest Is Sky High in This Euro Nation," *CNBC*, April 4, 2013, http://www.cnbc .com/id/100618694.

[132] Jan Jahosky, "BitPay Exceeds 1,000 Merchants Accepting Bitcoin," *BitPay Blog*, September 11, 2012, http:// blog.bitpay.com/2012/09/bitpay-exceeds-1000-merchants-accepting.html.

In: Virtual Currency …
Editor: Valerie Duskin

ISBN: 978-1-63117-280-9

Chapter 8

TESTIMONY OF ERNIE ALLEN, PRESIDENT AND CEO, THE INTERNATIONAL CENTRE FOR MISSING & EXPLOITED CHILDREN. HEARING ON "BEYOND SILK ROAD: POTENTIAL RISKS, THREATS, AND PROMISES OF VIRTUAL CURRENCIES"*

Mr. Chairman and distinguished members of the Committee, I welcome the opportunity to appear before you today to discuss the challenges and opportunities associated with the emerging digital economy. We are deeply grateful for the Committee's leadership on these issues and its long-standing commitment to the safety of our children.

The International Centre for Missing & Exploited Children ("ICMEC") is a not-for-profit corporation, supported entirely by private funds and resources. ICMEC leads a global movement to protect children from sexual exploitation and abduction. We have

- Trained law enforcement in 121 countries;
- Reviewed laws in 200 countries and worked with parliaments in 100 countries to enact new law on child pornography.

---

* This is an edited, reformatted and augmented version of a testimony, presented November 18, 2013 before the Senate Committee on Homeland Security and Governmental Affairs.

- Reviewed laws in 200 countries, developed model law on child sexual exploitation, and worked with parliaments and international bodies to change national legislation and international conventions.
- Created a research institute, the Koons Family Institute on International Law & Policy, to examine child abduction and sexual exploitation and launch policy initiatives with world leaders.
- Built a Global Missing Children's Network, now including 22 countries.
- Worked with Belgium, Romania, South Africa, Russia, Belarus and others to establish national centers on missing & exploited children.
- Created a regional center, the Southeastern European Center on Missing and Exploited Children, serving thirteen countries in the Balkan region.
- Entered into formal partnerships with Interpol, the Organization of American States, the Hague Conference on Private International Law, and others.
- Hosted international conferences, including a 2009 meeting of 400 Arab leaders in Cairo which produced "The Cairo Declaration," an agreement on child protection; a 2010 conference of judges from 15 countries at the US State Department to examine cross-border transportation of children, resulting in the "The Washington Declaration," now cited in case law worldwide; and a 2011 forum in Rome in partnership with the Vatican, the Mayo Clinic and Il Telefono Azzurro, which produced "The Declaration of Rome" on children's rights.
- Managed private sector financial industry and technology industry coalitions to address child sexual exploitation.
- Launched a Global Health Coalition of pharmaceutical companies and health care institutions to attack the problem of child sexual abuse and exploitation not just from a legal and law enforcement perspective but as a public health crisis.
- And there is much more.

I am honored to have the opportunity to address the risks and the promise of virtual currencies. We are enthusiastic about the potential of virtual currencies and the digital economy. We believe that the digital economy can achieve social good, particularly in bringing about real financial inclusion for the 2.5 billion adults on the planet today without access to banks, credit cards or the mainstream financial system. In addition, a digital economy is attractive to tech-centric young people, and has particular appeal in light of the global movement to mobile technologies and mobile payment systems.

Nonetheless, the International Centre for Missing & Exploited Children is involved in this issue because there are risks. For the past year I have consulted with law enforcement and financial experts worldwide. While much of the evidence is still anecdotal, there is consensus that commercial child pornography, sexual exploitation, sex trafficking and other criminal enterprises are increasingly moving to a new unregulated, unbanked digital economy. Through voluntary industry coalitions and following the money through the trails and tunnels of the payments system, these enterprises had declined dramatically. Yet, we have concluded that "we didn't end it, we just moved it."

There are three primary reasons for this migration: (1) anonymity; (2) the emergence of new, digital economy that belongs to no nation and is overseen by no central bank; and (3) most countries have not yet begun to apply existing laws and regulations to virtual currencies at the exchange level; i.e., the point at which virtual currencies are traded for dollars, euros, pounds, yen, etc. A US Treasury Department official told us, "the more virtual currencies function like real currencies, the greater the illicit finance threat." Yet, few countries are addressing this emerging threat.

There are positive signs. In March the Financial Crime Enforcement Network, or FinCEN, in the US issued guidance on the legal status of Bitcoin, the best-known digital currency, under the money laundering laws. Bitcoin exchanges, which exchange Bitcoins for conventional currencies, and most Bitcoin miners are required to register as Money Services Businesses and comply with anti-money laundering regulations. FinCEN indicated that a "money transmitter" is anyone that (1) "accepts and transmits a convertible virtual currency" or (2) "buys or sells convertible virtual currency for any reason." However, Bitcoin users who merely use the currency to purchase goods and services are not required to register. We believe that this is not only a positive step for the issues we are concerned about, it is also a positive step for Bitcoin.

In July the Financial Action Task Force (FATF), the 36-member, inter-governmental body based in Paris, issued similar guidance. The FATF focuses on combating money laundering and the financing of terrorism.

We define key elements of the digital economy as including digital currencies; anonymous online payment systems; anonymous Internet tools; and bulletproof hosting. A primary area of focus is digital currencies, particularly those with bidirectional flow; i.e., digital currencies which are bought and sold at prevailing exchange rates and used to purchase both real and virtual goods and services. The best-known example is Bitcoin.

As a result of our consultations with law enforcement leaders worldwide, ICMEC, in partnership with Thomson Reuters, the global media and information company, set out to find a balanced, reasonable response to the problems associated with the misuse of digital currencies for child sexual exploitation and other criminal activity. In June ICMEC and Thomson Reuters convened a conference on this issue and also met with global financial leaders at the World Bank. As a result we created a Digital Economy Task Force, which includes the Bitcoin Foundation, the Tor Project, the Gates Foundation, the Brookings Institution, the Cato Institute, Vital Voices, law enforcement leaders and others. Our goal is to offer recommendations and real solutions for the threats and risks without jeopardizing the promise and potential of the digital economy.

You asked that I address several questions:

1) The extent to which virtual currencies are being used directly in child-exploitive or related online criminal activities, or in support of such activities;
2) The unique challenges that virtual currencies bring for law enforcement investigations and prosecutions; and
3) The work of our Digital Economy Task Force and other collaborative efforts;
4) Future trends and potential policy considerations for Congress and other policymakers.

1. The Use of Virtual Currencies in Child-Exploitive or Related Online Criminal Activities, or in Support of Such Activities

Great progress has been made in addressing the use of the mainstream payments system for commercial child sexual exploitation. Nonetheless, we are concerned about the apparent migration of commercial child sexual exploitation, including sex abuse images, child exploitation and sex trafficking, along with other criminal enterprises to a new unregulated digital economy, made up of digital currencies; anonymous online payment systems; anonymous internet tools; and file hosting companies.

While much of our evidence regarding the use of digital currencies in child exploitation is anecdotal, a leading law enforcement expert advised us that child pornography producers are using Tor hidden services for the creation and dissemination of child pornography and Bitcoin for payment. However, he cautioned that the market to buy/sell child pornography on Tor hidden services using Bitcoins is small in comparison to the market for drugs and other illegal goods. He called the use of Tor and digital currencies for child pornography “significant” because those involved are the actual producers of the content. Thus, these crimes tend to involve new victims whom law enforcement has not seen before, and creates the presumption that the abuse is likely to be on-going.

There is a twofold challenge for law enforcement: the anonymity provided by Tor and the complexities of Bitcoin. The attractiveness of Tor and Bitcoin for child pornography is based upon a perception of anonymity. Those who use Tor and Bitcoin sacrifice speed for anonymity. Thus, if the perception of anonymity diminishes, we believe the criminal use will diminish with it.

In August 2013 the Irish founder/owner/operator of Freedom Hosting, which the FBI called “the largest facilitator of child pornography on the planet,” was arrested. Freedom Hosting maintained servers for a number of Tor-based, so-called “deep web” child pornography sites and others. The best –known child pornography sites included Lolita City, the Love Zone and PedoEmpire, all of which accept Bitcoins for payment.

To shut down Freedom Hosting, law enforcement exploited a “java script exploit,” a vulnerability in the site, enabling law enforcement to penetrate Tor and expose the IP addresses of the users of Freedom Hosting. Interestingly, in 2011 the hacktivist group, Anonymous, hacked into Tor to shut down Lolita City. However, Lolita City has reemerged with an estimated 15,000 members and 1.5 million child pornography images.

The digital economy of today is centered on peer-to-peer networks. There is clear evidence of the movement of child pornography and other types of exploitation from Internet Service Providers and central servers to peer-to-peer networks. Law enforcement is having some success in identifying individual users through the use of specialized peer-to-peer investigative tools to penetrate p2p-based operations. Yet, the emergence of a p2p-based digital economy is posing enormous challenges.

Much of the current discussion about digital currencies centers on Bitcoin, which can be bought and sold at prevailing exchange rates and then used to purchase both real and virtual goods and services. It is different from other digital currencies which may be purchased at a specific exchange rate, but may not be exchanged back. Examples are Facebook credits, Amazon coins, or frequent flyer points.

Recently, a judge in Texas ruled that Bitcoin is a currency. He compared it to a precious metal. Today, there are Bitcoin exchanges, like Mt. Gox in Japan, where one can exchange Bitcoins for conventional currencies. All Bitcoin transactions are visible and transparent. The challenge for law enforcement is in going from those transactions to an actual person.

It is not my position that Bitcoin or the emergence of a digital economy is negative. Nonetheless, there are challenges.

2. The Unique Challenges That Virtual Currencies Bring for Law Enforcement Investigation and Prosecution

The primary challenge facing law enforcement worldwide today is the growing anonymity surrounding internet transactions and the emergence of a so-called "deep web." In its April 24, 2012 Intelligence Estimate focusing on Bitcoin, ("Bitcoin Virtual Currency: Unique Features Present Distinct Challenges for Deterring Illicit Activity"), the FBI reported, "Bitcoin...provides a venue for individuals to generate, transfer, launder and steal illicit funds with some anonymity. Bitcoin offers many of the same challenges associated with other virtual currencies, such as WebMoney, and adds unique complexities for investigators because of its decentralized nature."

The FBI report adds, "Since Bitcoin does not have a centralized authority, law enforcement faces difficulties detecting suspicious activity, identifying users, and obtaining transaction records – problems that might attract malicious actors to Bitcoin. Bitcoin might also logically attract money launderers and other criminals who avoid traditional financial systems by using the internet to conduct global money transfers."

All of this is exacerbated by the emergence of Tor, The Onion Router, created by the US government to enable political dissidents to use the internet anonymously, avoiding retaliation from repressive regimes. It is a noble, high-minded, laudable purpose, and it protects not only political dissidents, but also journalists in countries where the practice of journalism is dangerous, victims of domestic violence or stalking, and others.

However, there are unintended consequences. Political dissidents, journalists and stalking victims are not the only ones using Tor. A March 6, 2013 headline in *Business Insider* read, "There's A Secret Internet For Drug Dealers, Assassins and Pedophiles." We are particularly concerned about the emergence of an unregulated "deep web" utilizing anonymizing hidden services and digital currencies for payment.

The so-called "deep web" made possible by anonymizing tools includes sites like Silk Road, but it also includes sites for the purchase of weapons; counterfeit currencies; assassins; stolen credit cards, fake IDs, and fake passports; and of particular concern to ICMEC, sites like Hard Candy, Jailbait, Lolita City, PedoEmpire, Love Zone and others for child abuse images. All of those sites accept digital currencies for payment.

It is important to note that while the so-called "deep web" is most often associated with Tor, Tor is not the only network being used or being developed to guarantee anonymity and untraceable access. In fact, there are indications that efforts are accelerating globally to create even more anonymous, impenetrable technologies.

In addition to Tor, there are the other "darknets," the Invisible Internet Project (I2P) and Freenet, and alternative top-level domains which are also called "rogue TLDs." I2P was designed as an anonymous peer-to-peer distributed communications layer that can run any traditional internet service. It was an evolution of the Freenet network. I2P's exclusive goal is to enable users to host services without being traceable or identifiable.

From consulting with law enforcement worldwide, it is clear there is progress. The recent arrest of the founder of Silk Road, "the Amazon for Drugs," was an important step. Yet, barely one month later the site is back up and is operating again.

There have been other arrests. In February Australian police arrested a cocaine dealer operating on Silk Road and being paid in Bitcoins. In May Israeli police broke up a drug distribution ring operating in Bitcoins. There have been others.

However, what I hear most from law enforcement worldwide is frustration. The primary investigative technique being utilized by police today for addressing anonymous, "deep web," criminal enterprises is infiltration. However, infiltration is expensive, time-consuming and often ineffective.

While there are some arrests, they primarily involve less sophisticated users who make mistakes and leave a trail. Even the Silk Road arrest appears to be largely the result of a series of mistakes by the offender. That doesn't minimize its importance or denigrate the incredible work of law enforcement to make it happen. Law enforcement must be vigilant and positioned to take advantage of the mistakes. It simply illustrates how daunting the challenge is.

In 2013 researchers at the University of Massachusetts reported that "while Tor presents a challenge to investigators, in practice offenders use Tor inconsistently. Over 90% of regular Tor users send traffic from a non-Tor IP at least once after first using Tor." Thus, most cases are currently being made due to mistakes by the offender. Our concern is that most often we are apprehending the less sophisticated offenders, not the serious, sophisticated organized criminals who represent the greatest threat and do not make these kinds of mistakes.

The Tor Project is committed to help train law enforcement in Tor technology, and should be praised for its willingness to help. It has also committed to help law enforcement develop ways to use Tor as part of its investigative arsenal. Nonetheless, it is vital that new investigative tools be developed.

We are also exploring some new techniques. For example, a recent analysis experimented with "clustering" Bitcoin transactions. While it is not possible to go from a transparent Bitcoin transaction to an actual human being, this analysis conducted by *Forbes Magazine* demonstrated that it is possible to identify patterns in Bitcoin transactions and to move from those patterns to the identification of specific offenders. The *Forbes* example unmasked the identities behind Bitcoin transactions on Silk Road.

Similarly, the recent investigation that shut down Freedom Hosting appeared to use variations of "hacking" techniques similar to those used by Anonymous in its efforts that shut down the child pornography site, Lolita City. These techniques offer potential for study, but must be examined carefully to ensure that legal and ethical standards are met.

Another concern is that in addition to the major "deep web" marketplaces like Silk Road, there are other sites that allow anonymous trading. According to an analysis by Digital Economy Task Force member, Trend Micro, there are underground message boards where people post and read generic classifieds regarding almost any good or service. There are also privately maintained sites that offer specific types of goods and services. Some are pages with prices and contact information for anonymous orders and others provide a full order and payment management system. Goods and services being offered include drugs, guns, hired assassins, child pornography, and much more.

TrendMicro concluded that the so-called "deep web" in general and Tor in particular offer a secure platform for cybercriminals to support a vast amount of illegal activities – from anonymous marketplaces to secure means of communications to an untraceable and difficult to shutdown infrastructure to deploy malware and botnets. It adds, "it becomes more important...to be able to track and monitor activities that take place in darknets, focusing today on Tor networks but extending in the future to other technologies."

3. The Work of the Digital Economy Task Force

On June 13, 2013 ICMEC and Thomson Reuters hosted a conference with leaders of the Bitcoin movement, the Tor Project, government and law enforcement experts, private sector leaders, and others. Speakers included the US State Department's Ambassador who heads the Trafficking in Persons Office, an executive from the World Bank, the US Justice Department's Chief of the Child Exploitation & Obscenity Section, the US Department of Homeland Security's head of its Blue Campaign on human trafficking, an official from the State Department's International Narcotics & Law Enforcement (INL) bureau, a Deputy Assistant Attorney General, and the Director of the US Financial Crimes Enforcement Network (FinCEN). The conference also included private sector leaders from Thomson Reuters, General Electric Co., TrendMicro and others.

The representatives of Bitcoin, Tor and other entities explained their systems and indicated a desire to work with ICMEC, Thomson Reuters and others to ensure that their services are not used for child exploitation, human trafficking and other criminal purposes. They argued that the new digital economy represents an historic opportunity to advance financial inclusion and that the use of their systems for child sexual exploitation harms their larger purpose. They committed to work with us to seek solutions.

On June 14, 2013 ICMEC and Thomson Reuters participated in a meeting at the World Bank with officials of the International Monetary Fund, the European Central Bank, the US Federal Reserve, the US Department of Treasury's Office on Terrorist Financing and Financial Crimes, and others. I presented our concerns that digital currencies and the digital economy were becoming safe havens for child pornography, sexual exploitation and sex trafficking, in addition to other criminal enterprises.

The European Central Bank cited four primary conclusions:

1) that virtual currencies do not yet pose a risk to price stability nor jeopardize financial stability;
2) that since they are not yet regulated and not closely supervised or overseen by any public authority, they pose a risk for users;
3) that they fall within the realm of central banks' authority as a result of characteristics shared with payment systems; and
4) that they represent "a challenge for authorities, as they might be used by criminals, fraudsters, and money launderers."

The ECB committed to monitor developments, set payments security requirements, keep legal frameworks updated and "facilitate a social dialogue."

The US Federal Reserve raised several questions:

a) Is Bitcoin a more efficient currency for illegal activities than physical currency?
b) (b) How anonymous is it?
c) How vulnerable is Bitcoin to theft and counterfeiting? Like cash, there is no recourse for a victim of theft. Is it easier to steal virtual currency or physical currency?
d) How vulnerable are Bitcoin exchanges to cyber attacks? This introduces volatility to the value of the currency.
e) Will other virtual currencies emerge to challenge Bitcoin?
f) Will Bitcoin or another virtual currency become "widespread enough to have implications for central bank currency and monetary policy?"; and
g) "Will bank-like institutions emerge to take deposits and make loans of virtual currencies?"

The Federal Reserve also committed to monitor the situation.

Thus, as a result of the June conference and subsequent meetings and consultations, in August ICMEC and Thomson Reuters created a Digital Economy Task Force to seek reasonable, constructive solutions, including best practices models to address the challenge of anonymity.

ICMEC also committed to launch a global advocacy effort to urge individual nations and international bodies to begin applying anti-money laundering rules and regulations at the exchange level; to engage international law enforcement partners in an effort to increase awareness of the risks of the digital economy and develop specialized investigative techniques for addressing these kinds of crimes; and initiate discussions with policy makers regarding the use of "money transmitter" laws, which are in place in almost every country but are currently not being used to address this growing problem.

The Digital Economy Task Force created five working groups: Defining the Problem; Regulation; Law Enforcement; Human Rights/Financial Inclusion; and Interagency Cooperation and Coordination. Each group is compiling specific recommendations, which will be reviewed by the full task force. The Task Force is committed to issuing its final report and findings by February 2014.

4. Future Trends and Potential Policy Considerations for Congress and Other Policymakers

The digital economy is an evolving field. The pace of innovation will quicken. There will be new technologies and new currencies. The intensity of the effort to achieve total internet anonymity will also increase, posing increasing challenges for law enforcement.

What can Congress do?

You can ensure that we apply and utilize existing law and regulation, and that we focus our regulatory attention at the point at which virtual currencies are being exchanged for conventional currencies.

You can help ensure global cooperation and coordination. Digital economy funds flow globally, network to network, not nation to nation. This is not a problem that the US government can solve alone. An excellent model is the recent US-led investigation that shut down Liberty Reserve, the Costa Rican company indicted for unlicensed money transmissions; i.e., laundering $6 billion in illicit funds, some of which came from the sale of child pornography. Seventeen nations participated in that investigation.

We are gratified by the work of US and international law enforcement in the fight against Internet-based child sexual exploitation. Entities like the Virtual Global Task Force, which brings together national law enforcement agencies in 12 nations including international bodies Interpol and Europol, and the Global Alliance Against Child Sexual Abuse Online, launched recently by the US and Europe which now has nearly 50 member countries, are great models for international cooperation. We need a quick, nimble response system. These are global crimes and require a global solution.

You can ensure that the response of government to this fragile, emerging area is not so draconian that the effect is simply to push these new enterprises outside the United States to countries where there is little or no regulation.

Finally, you can help us address the core challenge, internet anonymity. For all of its importance, we simply cannot create an environment in which child exploiters, traffickers, and other organized criminals can operate on the internet with a complete veil of anonymity and no risk of being identified unless they make a mistake.

In our consultations with law enforcement worldwide, we have heard the argument that there is a difference between privacy and anonymity. Law enforcement leaders embrace the broadest possible privacy protections for individuals, but emphasize that absolute internet anonymity is a prescription for catastrophe.

Our challenge is to find the right balance. Free speech is not absolute. Nearly a century ago, the US Supreme Court articulated the "clear and present danger" test, emphasizing that limits on speech may be appropriate based upon the context in which that speech is exercised.

That determination is much more difficult today in the world of the internet, a medium that is global in scope. We recognize that protecting the rights of political dissidents, journalists and others is incredibly important. We also recognize that all countries are not equally committed to individual freedoms, and that there are countries which will use internet speech as a basis for retaliation.

Nonetheless, the crux of the challenge we face with regard to the use of the digital economy for the exploitation and victimization of children and other criminal purposes is internet anonymity. There have to be some limits, hopefully as minimal as possible. Law enforcement has to have some possibility of tracing evidence of unlawful behavior, with full and appropriate legal processes, to the person responsible for it.

In her "Remarks on Internet Freedom" at the Newseum in Washington, DC in January 2010, former Secretary of State Hillary Clinton said, "On the one hand, anonymity protects the exploitation of children. And on the other hand, anonymity protects the free expression of opposition to repressive governments." That is our challenge.

Secretary Clinton added, "...we must grapple with the issue of anonymous speech. Those who use the internet to recruit terrorists or distribute stolen intellectual property cannot divorce their online actions from their real world identities. But these challenges must not become an excuse for governments to systematically violate the rights and privacy of those who use the internet for peaceful political purposes."

She added, "None of this will be easy...But I think these overriding principles should be our guiding light. We should err on the side of openness and do everything possible to create that, recognizing, as with any rule or any statement of principle, there are going to be exceptions."

She was exactly right. We must develop and implement those limited exceptions.

In: Virtual Currency …
Editor: Valerie Duskin
ISBN: 978-1-63117-280-9

Chapter 9

Statement of Anthony Gallippi, CEO, BitPay. Hearing on "The Present and Future Impact of Virtual Currency"*

Thank you Chairmen Merkley and Warner, and Ranking Members Heller and Kirk, and Distinguished Members of the Committees for the opportunity to speak with you today.

My name is Tony Gallippi and I am the Co-founder and CEO of BitPay. I graduated magna cum laude from Georgia Tech with a degree in Mechanical Engineering. BitPay is a startup company with sixteen full-time employees, based in Atlanta.

I appreciate the Members for their interest in the commercial and international trade uses of digital currencies, and more importantly, the opportunities for digital currencies to create jobs in America and to increase America's exports. Since Bitcoin represents the dominant market share of virtual currencies, my testimony will focus on Bitcoin specifically and not on any of the alternative virtual currencies.

Our company BitPay was started in May 2011 and we have been operating for over two years now, which makes us pretty old in the Bitcoin space. During this time we have acquired over 12,000 merchants to accept bitcoin with our service. Our merchants include many small and medium-sized businesses in every State, who accept bitcoin side-by-side with credit cards and other forms of payment.

* Presented November 19, 2013 before the Senate Committee on Banking, Housing, and Urban Affairs, Subcommittee on National Security and International Trade and Finance.

Most online payments today are made with credit cards, but credit cards were never designed for the Internet. Credit cards were designed in the 1950's, and they still function the pre-internet age. Last year, over 12 million people became victims of identity theft, mostly from shopping online (source: https://www.javelinstrategy.com/news/1387/92/1). Businesses lose over $20 billion per year due to payment fraud (source: http://www.lexisnexis.com/risk /downloads/assets/true-cost-fraud-2013.pdf). The banks don't take responsibility for the fraud. If you are a business owner, it is your fault that you took a stolen credit card, even if the bank approved it. Credit Card fees are discriminatory - the highest fees are paid by the smallest mom-and-pop businesses and the lowest income consumers. Bitcoin is a cheaper, faster, and more secure payment system.

Background on Merchant Acquiring

Even though we deal with bitcoin, our business model of merchant acquiring is fairly traditional. Merchant Acquiring began in the 1950s with credit cards, and the big marketing push to get businesses to accept credit cards as payment. Over the years, companies such as First Data, TSYS, Fiserv, and others would emerge with new tools for merchants. These companies are typically not household names. They operate behind the scenes, facilitating merchant payment acceptance as a business-to-business service. Most consumers, even when making a payment through one of these service providers, don't even know that these companies exist.

Fast forward 40 years to the 1990's with the launch of the world wide web and the first web browser. Businesses could build a website to reach customers, but how could they take a payment from a web page? It was the mail-order companies who figured it out first. If they could accept a credit card over the phone, then perhaps they could also accept a credit card over the internet. Companies like Cybersource and Authorize.net built payment gateways for processing credit cards over the internet, and today, 20 years later, credit cards are still the most widely used form of payment over the internet.

DIFFERENCES BETWEEN CREDIT CARDS AND BITCOIN

Credit cards are "pull" transactions. The shopper provides their account number, and secret credentials that the business can use to pull money from their account. The problem is that the same credentials to pull money one time can be used to pull money many more times - by that same business, or by anyone who has these credentials. This is the fundamental design problem with credit cards, and it is the root cause of the identity theft and fraud that we see today.

Think about that for a minute. Why would you ever give someone full access to your $20,000 line of credit to pay them 20 dollars?

Because of this design flaw, security around credit cards is massively expensive. Apple has iTunes, with over 500 million credit card numbers stored on file. The cost and risk of securing this data is enormous. Visa alone spends $200 million a year on fraud prevention. They are throwing big money at the problem and it is not working, because every year fraud remains very high.

In 2009, Bitcoin was invented. Bitcoin takes everything we know about the Internet, Security, and Cryptography, and builds a payment system designed for the Internet.

Bitcoin is an open standard, an open protocol, and an open source payment network. Nobody owns the network, and nobody controls the network. All of the users collectively own the network, its rules, and its ledger.

Anyone can use bitcoin or build an application on top of bitcoin. Bitcoin is much like the Internet itself, where anyone can use the Internet and build an application on top of the Internet. And because bitcoin is borderless, a business can receive a payment from China just as easily as they can receive it from someone in the same room.

Bitcoin payments are "push" transactions, which are very different than credit cards. If I want to pay someone, I push them the exact amount I want to give them. The recipient does not get my account number, they do not get my secret credentials, and they do not get any permission to ever pull money from my account. Only I can push out a payment. Bitcoin works similar to email, and text messages. Text messages are a push transaction. You cannot pull an email from me or a text message from me, only I can push the message to you. Bitcoin works the same way, for payments.

BITPAY IS A BITCOIN MERCHANT ACQUIRER

At BitPay, our role in the bitcoin ecosystem is very close to that of the traditional merchant acquirers in the credit card space. We act as an agent of the payee, to help merchants clear and settle transactions over the bitcoin network. Merchants could accept bitcoin directly, but automating this is very difficult, and most merchants choose to use our software and service rather than try to figure it out themselves.

BitPay has a strict Know Your Customer (KYC) policy to verify all of our merchant applications. We need to know who our merchants are and what they are selling. We only want the good actors using our service. We routinely audit our merchants, and we suspend and terminate those who violate our Terms of Use. A copy of BitPay's Merchant Terms of Use is attached in Exhibit A.

BitPay also follows all Bank Secrecy Act (BSA) guidelines to prevent, detect, and report suspicious activity. Our strict policies to comply with laws and protect our brand have earned BitPay the reputation as a leader and well-respected company in the payments space.

BitPay is not a bitcoin exchange, but we use nearly all of the bitcoin exchanges around the world to manage our own asset allocation. We do not act as a broker dealer to facilitate trades, and we also do not offer any bitcoin services for consumers. Consumers do not need to store funds with BitPay, they can simply pay the merchant invoice from whichever bitcoin wallet they choose to push the payment from. In the near future, our service will be more integrated into the merchants branding and checkout experience.

BITCOIN PROTECTS CONSUMERS FROM IDENTITY THEFT

For consumers, Bitcoin is another choice of payment which is voluntary to use. One of the main reasons why a consumer would choose to pay with Bitcoin is that Bitcoin can reduce, if not completely eliminate, the risk of the consumer becoming a victim of identity theft. Identity theft happens when a criminal gets access to the victim's account number and credit card credentials, and uses those credentials to make unauthorized purchases. When using Bitcoin, the consumer never needs to provide their identity to make a payment, so there is no identity information to steal, and no risk of identity theft. Bitcoin is a massive win for consumers, saving 12 million people per year the expense and hassle of dealing with the fallout of identity theft.

Consumers will be educated of the different ways in which they store their bitcoin. It functions more like cash, where if you lose it, it's gone. The funds are locked in the private key, which defines the ownership of the asset. Consumers can create many wallets with varying levels of convenience and security. The technology is being developed, and consumers will be educated on data security and proper data backups to ensure proper use of the technology. If consumers understand how bitcoin works, they should be allowed to use it.

BITCOIN PROTECTS BUSINESSES FROM PAYMENT FRAUD

For businesses, Bitcoin can also stop the $20 billion/year fraud problem. When your business receives a bitcoin payment, it's confirmed, and it's yours. It cannot be reversed or taken away from you. Businesses can now reach customers in emerging markets, where they could not collect payments from before.

Credit cards for online businesses don't really work beyond 8 or 10 countries, so most businesses simply choose not to sell internationally - not because their website can't reach, or their shipping company can't reach, but only because they can't take the payment.

It is the small mom-and-pop businesses that are most excited about bitcoin, and represent most of the adoption today. The businesses who accept bitcoin are now opening up new markets, and creating more exports, and more jobs in America. If the United States doesn't allow our businesses to accept bitcoin and create more jobs and exports, then countries like Germany and China certainly will.

BITCOIN'S LIMITATIONS

Bitcoin does have limitations that will keep it a small player in the payments space for quite some time. Compared to credit cards, Visa's payment network can handle 20,000 transactions per second, worldwide. Bitcoin can handle seven.

Not seven thousand, but seven transactions per second. Today, the average rate on the bitcoin network is one transaction per second. So compared to the collective networks of credit cards, debit cards, payment cards, ACH, and wires, there are 50,000 times more transactions taking place on traditional networks than on the bitcoin network.

Bitcoin also has some limitations on its usability. The global money supply of bitcoin is worth around $5 billion. Compare this with the global M2 money supply of around $70 trillion, there is 15,000 times more money in the world in traditional currencies than in bitcoin.

BITCOIN'S POTENTIAL FOR NON-MONETARY USE

Even though it's small, Bitcoin has invented something previously thought to be impossible. Many times when parties transfer assets to each other, they are trading a digital representation of an asset. The asset itself settles 1-3 days later. With Bitcoin, it is now possible to transfer an asset remotely, and immediately settle the transaction, with no counterparty risk. That type of instrument has never existed before.

The possibilities of this instant worldwide settlement are very interesting. And this is where the real potential for Bitcoin exists. The Bitcoin blockchain, which is the public accounting ledger of bitcoin, is a large property rights database. It can handle quadrillions of individual asset accounts, with a full chain of custody every time an asset is transferred from one party to another party.

If you want to energize the housing market, think of bitcoin. The biggest up-front costs for consumers trying to buy a home are the closing costs, which include fees for deeds, titles, stamps, title insurance, and other redundant tasks to record the sale in different recordbooks. Bitcoin can replace thousands of dollars in closing costs with a single transaction that costs 5 cents. By reporting deeds and titles on the blockchain, the information would be public record forever, for pennies, and eliminate the need for title insurance.

The property rights aspect of Bitcoin can go one-step further, to create smart property. This can be used for purchases like cars, where if a loan is attached to the car, the ownership of the car can be transferred back to the lender in case of default, or if the loan is paid off the owner would have full ownership of the car, and then they can transfer it to whomever they want.

BITCOIN RISKS

Bitcoin does have risks. Criminals use cell phones, criminals use email, and criminals use dollars and banks. Many businesses like BitPay, offering innovative services ontop of bitcoin, share the Committee's goals to protect consumers from fraud, and keep the criminals away from our businesses.

The Board of Governors of the Federal Reserve System acknowledged that virtual currencies "may pose risks related to law enforcement and supervisory matters," but "there are also areas in which they may hold long-term promise, particularly if the innovations promote a faster, more secure and more efficient payment system."

BITCOIN REGULATION

Guidance from the IRS, Department of Treasury, Department of Justice, and SEC has all established that Bitcoins are legal, and that those dealing with them must simply follow existing tax laws and anti-money-laundering regulations.

In the 1990s when the Internet was in its infancy, Congress took a wait-and-see attitude to let the Internet develop. Where would Social Media and other free apps be today if in the 1990s we required licenses for the Internet, and taxed Internet access as if it was a Telecom?

In 1995, the National Science Foundation lifted its strict prohibition of commercial enterprise on the Internet, and immediately companies like Amazon, Ebay, and Dell were born. Americans will benefit from a similar openness and wait-and-see approach to Bitcoin.

BITCOIN REGULATION OUTSIDE THE UNITED STATES

Bitcoin by design is borderless, like the Internet itself. Businesses using bitcoin are forming every day, at a pace not seen since the expansion of the world wide web in the 1990s. There is a tremendous amount of capital, resources and effort being spent to create innovation in finance.

We don't believe that new legislation or regulation around bitcoin is needed. The rules for consumer protection and anti-money laundering already exist today.

Germany has declared Bitcoin to be "private money" and other countries are working to categorize Bitcoin and Bitcoin related services into regulatory frameworks that exist today. Bitcoin is a technology with tremendous cost savings for businesses and consumers. Bitcoin is a more secure, faster, and more affordable option for transferring funds. If America is the leader in Bitcoin technology, America will create more jobs and more exports.

BITCOIN IS DISRUPTIVE

Bitcoin is a disruptive technology. Bitcoin will not replace the dollar, or the euro, or gold, but it will certainly disrupt existing financial services and their fee structures. Today banks charge many fees to consumers: overdraft fees, overlimit fees, interest fees, application fees, monthly fees, authorization fees, processing fees, ATM fees, maintenance fees, minimum balance fees, late fees, and even fees to send your paper statement in the mail. With bitcoin, users can handle many of their daily payments needs themselves and avoid the bank fees, so banks relying on fee revenue could be impacted the most by virtual currencies.

Most IT systems used by banks and financial services today were built in the 1970s. They were designed well before the Internet and they lack many of the technical innovations that other industries use today. Bitcoin could offer immediate cost reductions and technical advancements to our financial institutions, particularly in the areas of interbank settlement, international transfers, and foreign exchange. The current 1-3 day settlement times on many types of transactions can be reduced to 1-3 seconds.

Bitcoin is a technology with tremendous cost savings for businesses and consumers. Bitcoin is a more secure, faster, and more affordable option for transferring funds. If America is the leader in Bitcoin technology, America will create more jobs and more exports.

CONCLUSION

In conclusion, today Bitcoin is in its infancy. It is much like the Internet in the early 1990s. Thanks to Congress's protection, the Internet was allowed to evolve and develop, and today it has greatly improved our lives.

If we look 10-20 years in the future, we will see many companies built upon bitcoin-related technology. We want those companies to be based in America, creating jobs in America, and building a revenue base and tax base in America.

The original application of the Internet was commerce, with companies like Amazon and Ebay. Over time, the killer apps for the Internet emerged, and these apps were not the original application. Search, Social Media, and Big Data are all powerful industries built on the Internet, and where would all of the free applications like Social Media be today if the early Internet was pigeonholed, overly regulated and required expensive telecom licenses?

I commend the Committee for recognizing the real, practical uses of virtual currencies and the potential future applications of this technology. Thank you for the opportunity to speak today.

Appendix A - BitPay Merchant Terms of Use

These Merchant Terms of Use (the Terms) govern your use of the products, services or any other features, technologies or functionalities (the Services) provided by BitPay, Inc. (BitPay, we, our, or us) through BitPay's website, API or through any other means. **You** and **your** mean the merchant to which we will be providing the Services and the person signing below or otherwise agreeing to the Terms on behalf of the merchant. Please read the Terms carefully; by using the Services, you agree to the Terms and confirm that you accept them.

The Services

We are a Bitcoin payment processor—we enable you to accept Bitcoins as payment for goods or services, and process Bitcoin payments that you receive from your customers. We are not a Bitcoin exchange, Bitcoin wallet, or a place to purchase Bitcoin. By using the Services, you authorize us to receive, hold and disburse funds on your behalf and to take any and all actions that we think are necessary or desirable to provide the Services and to comply with applicable law.

Registration

Generally

In order to use the Services, you must open a BitPay account. When you open an account, we will ask you for contact information such as, for instance, your name, mailing address, phone number, email address, and website. The information that you provide at the time of account opening must be accurate and complete, and you must inform us in a timely fashion of any changes to such information. We may require additional information about you (including any person signing below or otherwise agreeing to the Terms on behalf of the merchant) such as, for instance, your date of birth, tax identification number or government-issued identification, and we may also obtain information about you from third parties, such as credit bureaus and identity verification services. We have the right to reject your account registration, or to later close your BitPay account, if you do not provide us with accurate, complete and satisfactory information.

Merchant Tiers

BitPay imposes daily transaction processing limits on merchants. When you register for a BitPay account, you will be required to select the limit (the Tier) that will apply to your BitPay account, and to provide us with the documentation necessary to qualify for that Tier. A description of the Tiers, as well as a list of the documentation required to qualify for each, is available on our website. If your business is a High Risk category, as determined by BitPay, you will be required to qualify for the "Trusted" Tier in order to use the Services. We will not begin to process payments on your behalf until we have reviewed the documentation that you provide, in accordance with applicable law. If you wish to change to a Tier with a higher limit, you must provide us with the additional required documentation. We will not approve your request to change Tiers and permit you a greater processing volume unless and until we have reviewed your documentation to our satisfaction. Please also refer to Section 3.1, "Daily Transaction Volume; Tiers."

Guarding Your Password

You will choose a password when registering. You are responsible for maintaining the confidentiality of your password and account. You are fully responsible for all activities that occur using your password or account. Please notify us immediately of any unauthorized use of your password or account or any other breach of security. We will not be liable for any loss that you may incur as a result of someone else using your password or account, either with or without your knowledge. You may not use anyone else's password at any time.

Prohibited Accounts

Use of the Services is subject to the laws and regulations of the United States regarding the prevention of terrorist financing and anti-money laundering. You agree and acknowledge that your use of the Services would and will comport with such laws and regulations, including, without limitation, the sanctions programs administered by the Office of Foreign Assets Control of the United States Department of the Treasury.

Your Sales

Daily Transaction Volume; Tiers

You agree to adhere to the transaction processing limits applicable to your Tier. You agree that, if you exceed that limit, BitPay has the right to hold the over-the-limit funds until you have provided us with the additional documentation required to qualify for the next Tier, and until we have had the opportunity to review such documents. We will take additional measures if you exceed your limit. If you are a "Trusted" merchant, you may create an unlimited value of invoices (see Section 8.1), although you will only receive payments from us up to the specified limit. If you are not a "Trusted" merchant, you may not create a value of invoices that exceeds your specified limit.

Invoices and Records

You must keep all records needed for fulfilling the merchandise to the purchaser and providing any post-sale support to the purchaser. If the sale of the item requires any government registration of the sale, you are responsible for such registration.

Customer Verification

You are solely responsible for obtaining any information required of those who purchase your goods or services. For instance, if applicable law prohibits a sale to persons under the age of 18 years, you must ensure that a purchaser is at least 18 years of age. Similarly, if applicable law requires that a purchaser's identity be verified, you must verify the purchaser's identity. We will not be responsible for your failure to adequately verify your purchasers' identities or qualifications.

Representation and Warranties

Your use of the Services is subject to several important restrictions. Specifically, you represent and warrant to us that:

a) Your use of the Services will not contravene any applicable international, federal, state or local law or regulation, including applicable tax laws and regulations, and that your use of the Services will not violate the laws of the United States of America.
b) Your use of the Services will not relate to sales of (i) narcotics, research chemicals or any controlled substances, (ii) cash or cash equivalents, including derivatives, (iii) items that infringe or violate any copyright or trademark, (iv) ammunition, firearms, explosives, weapons or knives regulated under applicable law, or (v) any services which compete with BitPay.
c) Your use of the Services will not relate to transactions that (i) show the personal information of third parties in violation of applicable law, (ii) support pyramid or Ponzi schemes, matrix programs or other "get rich quick" schemes, (iii) are associated with purchases of annuities or lottery contracts, lay-away systems, off-shore banking or transactions to finance or refinance debts funded by a credit card, (iv) are associated with Money Service Business activities, as defined by the Financial Crimes Enforcement Network of the United States Department of the Treasury, or (v) provide credit repair or debt settlement services.
d) Your use of the Services will not involve gambling or any other activity with an entry fee and a prize, including, but not limited to casino games, sports betting, horse or greyhound racing, lottery tickets, other ventures that facilitate gambling, and sweepstakes, unless you have obtained our prior approval and you and your customers are located exclusively in jurisdictions where such activities are permitted by law.
e) You have the right, power and ability to enter into and perform under these Terms.

Our Right to Reject

We reserve the right to decline to process a sale if we believe that it violates these Terms or would expose you, other merchants, purchasers, or other parties to harm. If we reasonably suspect that your BitPay account has been used for an illegal purpose, you authorize us to share information about you, your BitPay account, and your account activity with law enforcement.

Our Right to Inspect

We may ask for permission to inspect your business location, in connection with your use of the Services or specific transactions. If you refuse our request, we may suspend or terminate your BitPay account.

Third Parties

Your Use of Third-Party Services

In using the BitPay website or the Services, you may be offered services, products and promotions provided by third parties. If you decide to use these third-party services, you do so at your own risk and are solely responsible for reviewing, understanding and complying with the associated terms and conditions. We expressly disclaim any liability for the third-party services and are not responsible for the performance of the third-party services or servicers.

Security

We have implemented security measures designed to secure your information from accidental loss and from unauthorized access, use, alteration or disclosure. However, we cannot guarantee that unauthorized persons will never gain access to your information, and you acknowledge that you provide your information at your own risk, except as otherwise provided by applicable law.

How We Collect, Use and Share Information

In order to provide the Services, we may share information about you and your BitPay account with third parties, including but not limited to your bank and purchasers.

Our Ownership of the Services and the BitPay Website

You agree and acknowledge that we own all right, title and interest to and in the Services, the associated software, technology tools and content, the

BitPay website, the content displayed on the website, and other materials produced by and related to BitPay (collectively, the BitPay IP). You are only permitted to use the Services and the BitPay IP to accept and receive payments, according to these Terms. When you accept the Terms, we grant you a personal, limited, revocable and non-transferable license to use the BitPay IP, without the right to sublicense. You shall not rent, lease, sublicense, distribute, transfer, copy, reproduce, download, display, modify or timeshare the BitPay IP or any portion thereof, or use the BitPay IP as a component of or a base for products or services prepared for commercial sale, sublicense, lease, access or distribution. You shall not prepare any derivative work based on the Company IP, nor shall you translate, reverse engineer, decompile or disassemble the Company IP.

Advertising

By mutual consent, we may publish your corporate name, artwork, text and logo **(Merchant Content)** on the BitPay website and promotional materials to acknowledge you as our customer. You represent and warrant to us that you have the right to provide the Merchant Content to us, and that the use, copying, modification and publication of the Merchant Content by us: (a) will not infringe, violate or misappropriate any third party copyright, patent, trade secret or other proprietary rights, (b) will not infringe any rights of publicity or privacy, and (c) will not be defamatory or obscene or otherwise violate any law.

Fees & Settlement

Invoice Generation and Exchange Rate Guarantee

To create an invoice, you may post a request to BitPay to collect a specific amount in your local currency, such as dollars or euros, or in Bitcoin. BitPay will pull the exchange rate and provide the Bitcoin payment instructions to the purchaser. We guarantee the exchange rate to you as long as the purchaser pays within the proper time window after the invoice is created. Invoice timeout information is clearly displayed on each BitPay invoice. While we guarantee the exchange rate as long as the purchaser pays within such time window, you agree that you assume the volatility risk of your local currency or Bitcoin, as applicable. For instance, if you ask us to collect USD $150, and the purchaser sends the payment within the time window, we guarantee you will receive exactly USD $150, minus our fee, but do not guarantee the value of the U.S. dollar.

Fees

We charge a processing fee on all transactions. The proceeds payable to you will equal the amount of the invoice (assuming that we have received the full amount of the invoice from the purchaser), unless you agree to accept less than the amount of the invoice, minus the processing fee. We reserve the right to change our fees and will give you 30 calendar days' prior notice of any fee increase. Your continued use of the Services after we notify you of any increase in our fees constitutes your acceptance of such change. Current pricing information is provided on the BitPay website at https://bitpay.com /pricing.

Methods of Settlement

We will clear the payments over the Bitcoin peer-to-peer payment network and post the balance to your accounting ledger, according to your preference settings. The debits and credits to your accounting ledger are funds temporarily held by BitPay until settlement to your bank account can take place. You can receive a settlement in your local currency, in Bitcoins, or in a mixture of both. You assume volatility risks of the currency in which you choose to be settled. If you choose to keep bitcoins, then you assume the volatility risk of the bitcoin value.

Settlements in Local Currencies

Direct deposit to a bank account in a local currency is available to merchants located in certain countries. Please refer to Please refer to https://bitpay.com/bitcoin-direct-deposit for a list of those countries. If you wish to receive direct deposit, you must provide us with valid bank account information and keep such information current. We will send a direct deposit to your bank account to clear out your accumulated balance. Minimum settlement amounts apply; please refer to https://bitpay.com/bitcoin-direct-deposit for information related to minimum settlement amounts and deposit frequency.

Your Bank Account

You must provide us with written notice at least 1 business day prior to closing your bank account. If you wish to continue to receive direct deposits, you must provide us with information for a substitute bank account. You are solely liable for all fees and costs associated with your bank account and for all overdrafts. You authorize us to initiate electronic credits to your bank account at any time, as necessary to process your transactions. We will not be liable for any delays in receipt of funds or errors in bank account entries caused by third parties.

Settlements in Bitcoins

Payments in Bitcoins are sent to the Bitcoin address of your choice, at least once per calendar day. BitPay does not operate a Bitcoin wallet and funds must be moved to your wallet address.

Certain Deferrals

If we need to conduct an investigation or resolve any pending dispute related to your BitPay account, we may delay settlement or restrict access to your funds while we do so. Additionally, we may delay settlement or restrict access to your funds if required to do so by law, court order or at the request of law enforcement.

Account Statements

On demand, we will provide you with a statement detailing your account transaction and settlement history. Should you identify an error in the statement, you must notify us of such error within 30 calendar days.

Refunds and Adjustments

Refund Procedures

In the event that you wish to issue a refund to a purchaser, BitPay can handle this. You can decide to issue a partial refund or the full amount of the initial purchase. You can also decide whether to issue the original amount of the invoice in your local currency or in the number of Bitcoins paid. If you do not have enough funds in your BitPay account to cover the refund, BitPay may require you to deposit Bitcoins into your BitPay account to cover the refund to the purchaser. Any required currency conversion during the refund process will be calculated at a spot rate determined by BitPay, following the guidelines found here: https://bitpay.com/bitcoin-exchange-rates.

Disclosure of Your Refund Policy

Merchants are required to have a clear refund policy for their customers. We recommend you refund the amount of the initial purchase in the currency in which the item was priced.

Purchaser Complaints

Purchasers filing complaints about a purchase will be forwarded to you for resolution. BitPay reserves the right to terminate accounts which receive excessive complaints.

Account Termination

Your Right to Close Your Account

You may close your BitPay account at any time. You will still be obligated to us for any fees incurred before the closure and we will remit to you funds not yet paid to you and associated with pre-closure sales. If your account balance is below our documented minimum transfer amount, you may be responsible for any transactions fees that may be incurred in the funds transfer.

Our Right to Close or Suspend Your Account

We may terminate these Terms and close your account, at our discretion, upon notice to you via email or phone communication. We may also suspend your access to the Services if we suspect that you have failed to comply with these Terms, pose an unacceptable fraud risk to us, or if you provide any false, incomplete, inaccurate or misleading information. We will not be liable to you for any losses that you incur in connection with our closure or suspension of your account.

Effect of Account Closure

If your BitPay account is closed, you agree: (a) to continue to be bound by these Terms, (b) to immediately stop using the Services, (c) that the license provided under these Terms shall end, (d) that we reserve the right (but have no obligation) to delete all of your information and account data stored on our servers, and (e) that we shall not be liable to you or any third party for termination of access to the Services or for deletion of your information or account data.

Indemnification

You agree to indemnify BitPay, its affiliated and related entities, and any of its officers, directors, employees and agents from and against any claims, costs, losses, liabilities, damages, expenses and judgments of any and every kind (including, without limitation, costs, expenses, and reasonable attorneys' fees) arising out of, relating to, or incurred in connection with any claim, complaint, action, audit, investigation, inquiry, or other proceeding instituted by a person or entity that arises or relates to: (a) any actual or alleged breach of your representations, warranties, or obligations set forth in these Terms; (b) your wrongful or improper use of the Services; (c) the products or services sold by you through the Services, including but not limited to any claims for false advertising, product defects, personal injury, death or property damage; or (d) any other party's access or use of the Services with your account information.

No Warranties

WE PROVIDE THE SERVICES ON AN "AS IS" AND "AS AVAILABLE" BASIS, AND YOUR USE OF THE SERVICES IS AT YOUR OWN RISK. TO THE MAXIMUM EXTENT PERMITTED BY APPLICABLE LAW, WE PROVIDE THE SERVICES WITHOUT WARRANTIES OF ANY KIND, WHETHER EXPRESS OR IMPLIED (INCLUDING, WITHOUT LIMITATION, WARRANTIES OF MERCHANTABILITY, FITNESS FOR A PARTICULAR PURPOSE, OR NON-INFRINGEMENT). WITHOUT LIMITING THE FOREGOING, WE DO NOT WARRANT THAT THE SERVICES (AND OUR WEBSITE): WILL OPERATE ERROR-FREE OR THAT DEFECTS OR ERRORS WILL BE CORRECTED; WILL MEET YOUR REQUIREMENTS OR WILL BE AVAILABLE, UNINTERRUPTED OR SECURE AT ANY PARTICULAR TIME OR LOCATION; ARE FREE FROM VIRUSES OR OTHER HARMFUL CONTENT. WE DO NOT ENDORESE, WARRANT, GURANTEE OR ASSUME RESPONSIBILITY FOR ANY PRODUCT OR SERVCE OFFERED OR ADVERTISED BY A THIRD PARTY THROUGH THE SERVICES OR THROUGH OUR WEBSITE, AND WE WILL NOT BE A PARTY TO NOR MONITOR ANY INTERACTIONS BETWEEN YOU AND THIRD-PARTY PROVIDERS OF PRODUCTS OR SERVICES.

Limitation of Liability

IN NO EVENT WILL WE BE LIABLE TO YOU OR ANY THIRD PARTY FOR ANY DIRECT, INDIRECT, SPECIAL, INCIDENTAL, CONSEQUENTIAL, EXEMPLARY OR PUNITIVE DAMAGES OR ANY LOSS, THEFT, DISAPPEARANCE, OR DAMAGES FOR LOST PROFITS, LOST REVENUES, LOST DATA OR OTHER INTANGIBLE LOSSES THAT RESULT FROM THE USE OF, INABILITY TO USE, OR UNAVAILABILITY OF THE SERVICES, REGARDLESS OF THE FORM

OF ACTION AND WHETHER OR NOT WE KNEW THAT SUCH DAMAGE MAY HAVE BEEN INCURRED. IN NO EVENT WILL

WE BE LIABLE TO YOU OR ANY THIRD PARTY FOR ANY DAMAGE, LOSS OR INJURY RESULTING FROM HACKING, TAMPERING, VIRUS TRANSMISSION OR OTHER UNAUTHORIZED ACCESS OR USE OF THE SERVICES, YOUR BITPAY ACCOUNT, OR ANY INFORMATION CONTAINED THEREIN. IN NO EVENT WILL OUR LIABILITY FOR ANY DAMAGES ARISING IN CONNECTION WITH THE SERVICES EXCEED THE FEES EARNED BY US IN CONNECTION WITH YOUR USE OF THE SERVICES DURING THE 6 MONTH PERIOD IMMEDIATELY PRECEDING THE EVENT GIVING RISE TO THE CLAIM FOR LIABILITY. THE FOREGOING LIMITATIONS OF LIABILITY SHALL APPLY TO THE FULLEST EXTENT PERMITTED BY LAW IN THE APPLICABLE JURISDICTION.

Miscellaneous

Taxes

You are responsible for determining any and all taxes assessed, incurred, or required to be collected, paid, or withheld for any reason in connection your use of our software and services (Taxes). You also are solely responsible for collecting, withholding, reporting, and remitting correct Taxes to the appropriate tax authority. We are not obligated to, nor will we determine whether Taxes apply, or calculate, collect, report, or remit any Taxes to any tax authority arising from any transaction.

If in a given calendar year you receive (i) more than $20,000 in gross amount of payments and (ii) more than 200 payments, BitPay will report annually to the Internal Revenue Service, as required by law, your name, address, tax identification number (such as a social security number, or employer identification number), the total dollar amount of the payments you receive in a calendar year and the total dollar amount of the payments you receive for each month in a calendar year.

Privacy Policy

Please see our Privacy Policy for information regarding how we collect and use information. The Privacy Policy is part of these Terms, so please make sure that you read it.

Assignment

You may not transfer or assign these Terms, or any rights granted by these Terms. You agree and acknowledge that we may assign or transfer these Terms.

Severability

Should any provision of these Terms be determined to be invalid or unenforceable under any law, rule, or regulation, such determination will not affect the validity or enforceability of any other provision of this Agreement.

Waivers

Our failure to assert any right or provision in these Terms shall not constitute a waiver of such right or provision, and no waiver of any term shall be deemed a further or continuing waiver of such or other term.

Entire Agreement

These Terms, including the Privacy Policy referenced herein, represent the entire understanding between us and you with respect to the matters discussed. Headings are included for convenience only, and shall not be considered in interpreting these Terms.

Notices

You agree to accept communications from us in an electronic format, and agree that all terms, conditions, agreements, notices, disclosures or other communications that we provide to you electronically will be considered to be "in writing."

Governing Law; Arbitration

These Terms will be governed by and construed in accordance with the laws of the State of Georgia without reference to conflict of law or choice of law provisions, and applicable federal law (including the Federal Arbitration Act). If a disagreement or dispute in any way involves the Services or these Terms and cannot be resolved between you and us with reasonable effort, the disagreement or dispute shall be resolved exclusively by final and binding administration by the American Arbitration Association (AAA), and will be conducted before a single arbiter pursuant to the applicable Rules and Procedures established by the AAA. You agree that the arbitration shall be held in the State of Georgia, or at any other location that is mutually agreed upon by you and us. You agree that the arbiter will apply the laws of the State of Georgia consistent with the Federal Arbitration Act, and will honor and agree to all applicable statutes of limitation. You agree that, unless prohibited by law, there shall be no authority for any claims to be arbitrated on a class or representative basis, and arbitration will only decide a dispute between you and us. Arbitration proceedings must be initiated within 1 year after the disagreement or dispute arises. If any part of this Arbitration clause is later deemed invalid as a matter of law, then the remaining portions of this section shall remain in effect, except that in no case shall there be a class arbitration.

Amendment

We may update or change these Terms from time to time. Except as otherwise provided in these Terms, we will notify you of any changes by electronic mail or by posting a link to the amended Terms on our website. If you continue to use the Services after we provide notice of such changes, your continued use constitutes an acceptance of the amended Terms and an agreement to be bound by them. If you do not agree to the amended Terms, you must close your BitPay account and discontinue your use of the Services.

Force Majeure

Neither you nor we will be liable for delays in processing or other nonperformance caused by such events as fires, telecommunications, utility, or power failures, equipment failures, labor strife, riots, war, nonperformance of our vendors or suppliers, acts of God, or other causes over which the respective party has no reasonable control; provided that the party has procedures reasonably suited to avoid the effects of such acts.

Survival

The provisions of Sections 2.2, 3.3, 3.4, 4.2, 5, 6, 7, 8.1, 8.5, 8.7, 8.8, 9 (including all subsections), 11, 12, 13, and 14.7 shall survive the termination of these Terms.

You agree that the person signing below has the authority to sign the Terms and to bind you, and you acknowledge and agree that you: (a) have read and understand the Terms; (b) intend to form a legally binding contract; and (c) will abide by all the Terms.

In: Virtual Currency …
Editor: Valerie Duskin
ISBN: 978-1-63117-280-9

Chapter 10

TESTIMONY OF MERCEDES KELLEY TUNSTALL, PARTNER AND PRACTICE LEADER, PRIVACY AND DATA SECURITY GROUP, BALLARD SPAHR LLP. HEARING ON "THE PRESENT AND FUTURE IMPACT OF VIRTUAL CURRENCY"*

INTRODUCTION

Chairman Merkley, Ranking Member Heller, and the Members of the Subcommittee, I am Mercedes Kelley Tunstall, a Partner at Ballard Spahr LLP and the Practice Leader of our firm's Privacy and Data Security Group. My testimony today reflects my personal experience with the virtual currency industry and represents my own opinion. My testimony does not necessarily reflect the opinions of Ballard Spahr LLP or our clients.

Thank you for this opportunity to testify about the present and future impact of virtual currency. I work directly with multiple clients that offer their own forms of virtual currency. I also advise large banking clients on how to interact with virtual currencies as well as how to structure their programs and services as to avoid being treated as virtual currency. I have spoken extensively on this topic during webinars and other public forums, and I have

* This is an edited, reformatted and augmented version of a testimony, presented November 19, 2013 before the Senate Committee on Banking, Housing, and Urban Affairs, Subcommittee on National Security and International Trade and Finance.

been quoted frequently by the press. I will focus my remarks today on the important steps that the virtual currency industry and federal regulators should take in order for virtual currency to have a commercially viable future.

The Next Generation of Virtual Currency

In only a few short years, Bitcoin may have become the most well-known virtual currency today, but Bitcoin has also demonstrated a number of weaknesses that the next generation of virtual currency should be careful to address.

I. Bitcoin ≠ Integration

Bitcoin has built its reputation and structured its virtual currency around being both antigovernment and anti-establishment. Although this reputation may be attractive to a certain type of consumer, the structure has limited, and will continue to limit, Bitcoin's adoption by a wider population. Due to Bitcoin's reputation, large financial institutions view the currency as being unreliable and therefore not able to meet their safety and soundness requirements. If a virtual currency could be reliable, then financial institutions may very well incorporate the currency as a solution to certain problems faced. For example, virtual currency could be attractive to large financial institutions if the fees associated virtual currency transactions, including the exchange fees, are lower than the fees accompanying other payments methods (e.g., interchange fees). The next generation of virtual currency should figure out a way to better align with existing payment methods, or virtual currency will never be able to move from a "niche" into the mainstream.

II. Virtual Currency ≠ Anonymity

One of the most frequently cited advantages of virtual currency is the increased privacy and anonymity associated with using Bitcoins. However, even Bitcoin is not completely anonymous as a public record of each Bitcoin transaction is electronically recorded. In order for the industry to continue maturing, the next generation of virtual currencies should dispel the perception that an important element of using virtual currency is the ability for an individual to engage in online transactions with complete anonymity.

In a transaction involving hard currency, the two parties to the transaction may not know each other, but in order for the currency to be handed from one person to the next, the two people must see each other and be in each other's presence (or have a proxy to do the same for them). This transaction is hardly anonymous, and yet many have compared Bitcoin transactions to cash exchanges between strangers and referred to such exchanges as being anonymous.

Instead, the distinction is that such cash transactions can occur without being recorded by any financial system or government and without the involvement of middlemen such as banks. As such, Bitcoins, like cash, have been used in transactions to perpetrate fraud, money laundering, and other illegal activities.

Unlike hard currency, however, technological solutions could be developed to track the digital exchange of virtual currency so that the transaction is not conducted through a middleman. Bitcoin and other virtual currency providers have a responsibility to prevent criminal activity and to comply with anti-money laundering and other laws. The next generation of virtual currencies must address the ability of individuals to use virtual currency to engage in illegal activities anonymously or the Congress, the federal agencies, or the courts may take action, which could result in harmful consequences to the industry's overall growth.

III. Bitcoin = Commodity or Bitcoin ≠ Commodity

Bitcoin displays some features that allow Bitcoin to function like a commodity, such as the self-imposed limit of 21 million Bitcoins and the volatility of the value of Bitcoins.

However, Bitcoin does not presently comply with current securities or commodities laws and regulations. In order for banks to work with virtual currencies, those virtual currencies either need to comply with or protect against commoditization.

Unless the next generation of virtual currencies can resolve the question as to whether virtual currency should be considered a commodity, the industry will remain characterized by volatility. Without further stabilization, mainstream adoption of virtual currency remains unlikely.

Regulatory Certainty

As the virtual currency industry matures, regulatory certainty will also be needed to ensure a future for this industry.

I. Legal Definition of Virtual Currency

The virtual currency industry would benefit greatly from guidance from the federal government as to the legal definition of virtual currency. Although it is clear from the Legal Tender Cases of the 1870's and 1880's that virtual currencies can legally operate in the United States of America, it is unclear as to what regulations could and should apply to virtual currency. The Commodity Futures Trading Commission and the Securities Exchange Commission have both examined Bitcoin-related issues and determined that there are times when the currency operates as a commodity/security, but beyond that, there is no existing legal framework that addresses the unique features and functionality of virtual currency.

II. Financial Crimes Enforcement Network

Existing FinCEN guidance has offered much-appreciated guidance for the industry and related players, but as the industry continues to mature, additional guidance will be needed on how to integrate virtual currency into the existing financial ecosystem, especially with regard to compliance with anti-money laundering requirements.

III. Electronic Fund Transfer Act / Federal Reserve Board Regulation E

Currently, consumer protections contained in financial regulations such as the Electronic Funds Transfer Act and its implementing regulation, Regulation E, do not apply to virtual currencies. Therefore, unauthorized transactions involving virtual currency have no recourse – once the currency is gone, it is gone, just as surely as when someone swipes bills from a wallet. Due to the electronic nature of virtual currencies, consumers may not understand the reasons for the disparate protections conferred on the use of these disparate payment forms. If consumers are unable to embrace virtual currency as a safe, effective means to conduct online (and even offline) transactions, industry growth will be stalled.

CONCLUSION

Thank you again for the opportunity to testify on these important issues. I would also like to express my appreciation to your staff for all their assistance in preparing for this hearing. I would be happy to address any specific questions that the Members of the Subcommittee may have for me.

In: Virtual Currency …
Editor: Valerie Duskin
ISBN: 978-1-63117-280-9

Chapter 11

STATEMENT OF SARAH JANE HUGHES, UNIVERSITY SCHOLAR AND FELLOW IN COMMERICAL LAW, INDIANA UNIVERSITY MAURER SCHOOL OF LAW. HEARING ON "THE PRESENT AND FUTURE IMPACT OF VIRTUAL CURRENCY"*

Chairman Merkley and Chairman Warner, Ranking Members Heller and Kirk, and Honorable Members of the Subcommittees on Economic Policy and National Security and International Trade and Finance, I am honored to be here with you today to discuss virtual currencies.

Monitoring the developments in virtual currencies and taking a responsible approach to their regulation reflects their growing presence in domestic and international transactions. Recent negative publicity associated with law enforcement action against Silk Road and reports of the disappearance of bitcoin exchanges in China and the Czech Republic raises important public policy concerns.

* This is an edited, reformatted and augmented version of a statement, presented November 19, 2013 before the Senate Committee on Banking, Housing, and Urban Affairs, Subcommittee on National Security and International Trade and Finance.

PART I. RECOMMENDATIONS AND A ROADMAP TO THE BALANCE OF THIS TESTIMONY

The Committee has invited testimony on a variety of subjects that I have addressed in this prepared statement. I have a number of recommendations that pertain to the Committee's question.

My recommendations include:

1. Retain the current division of regulation between the States and Federal Government – with prudential regulation of the non-depository providers of new payments systems with the States and retaining the anti-moneylaundering, anti-terrorism and economic sanctions regulations with the Federal Government.
2. Make providers of virtual currencies comply with the customer-identification program and AML compliance program requirements of Sections 326 and 352 of the USA PATRIOT Act, and with the economic sanctions regulations enforced by OFAC, just as other payments systems providers do. Virtual currency customers will have to reveal their identities to issuers of the currencies they use. As a corollary, customers should get the same federal financial privacy rights that users of other payments products have under the Right to Financial Privacy Act of 1978 and Title V of the Gramm-LeachBliley Act.
3. Encourage FinCEN to clarify the manner in which customer-identification and AML compliance requirements apply to virtual currencies. This is needed to help banks ensure that they can do business with providers and users of virtual currencies and other payments innovators. Second-stage innovations from distributed computing and database technologies could offer benefits to payments and commerce far beyond those that virtual currencies now offer. If banks cannot determine how to comply with FinCEN regulations, for example, they may continue to terminate their relationships with payments innovators before the innovators can attract investors and users to make it to the second-stage technologies their current work may generate.
4. Encourage payments systems innovators to adopt and publicize transparent payment systems rules for their own systems and even to

compete for customers on the basis of the system rules they adopt. It is too early to enact user protections for virtual currencies.

5. Ignore the claims that
   a) additional regulation of virtual currencies will halt innovations,
   b) innovators deserve freedom from regulations that apply to other payments systems and their providers, and
   c) virtual currencies deserve a single federal licensure system that preempts State prudential regulation and licensure.
6. Monitor the development of virtual currency providers in case they transform their products into commodities or securities and, if this happens, then decide whether regulating their products under the applicable regulations makes more sense.
7. Leave room for non-depository and depository providers of payments products to innovate in the virtual currency space.
8. Authorize and fund a study of virtual currencies to be carried out by the Federal Reserve Board or pursuant to the Federal Advisory Committees Act by an inter-agency task force and industry participants.

The balance of this statement begins in Part II with a brief history of "legal tender" and the regulation of payments products in the United States. Part III discusses my recommendations in some greater detail. Part IV responds to questions posed in the Committee's invitation to testify.

PART II. A SHORT HISTORY OF "LEGAL TENDER" AND GOVERNMENTS' ROLES IN ESTABLISHING IT AND ITS VALUE

The emergence of a large digital "currency" unconnected to a sovereign threatens a sovereign right recognized back to Renaissance times. In one of the earliest court decisions involving "legal tender" – the 1605 decision in Britain of *The Case of Mixed Money*[1] in which the House of Lords observed that the regulation of currency was a sovereign right and declaring the sovereign's right to declare "legal tender" by decree, the affixing of the sovereign's stamp, and to decision of the value of increments of currency – and later to change its mind about valuation. "The prince, the stamp, and the value" became from that point forward hallmarks of what could pass as "legal tender" that participants in trade transactions were required by the sovereign to take from others in satisfaction of obligations (trade or debt) they undertook. Proponents of virtual currencies often seek to end sovereign "monopolies" over legal tender, fiat currencies.

Contributing to the history of sovereign, stamps, and values was the rambunctious, highly problematic period in the United States in the pre-Civil War 19th Century in which "wild cat" banks operated. Banks issued paper notes – a form of what economists call *fiat currencies* – as opposed to coins or other "specie." Persons who took paper "bank notes" encountered significant problems with redeeming the value that the notes were supposed to represent.[2] They either encountered long waits while the notes moved for collection from banks near them to distant issuers of these notes, additional long periods while the issuing bank assembled enough funds to pay them off, or were forced to take huge discounts from local depositary banks against the prospect of these long waits or insolvency when the notes were eventually presented for payment to their issuing banks. "Wild cat banking" was cited as a cause of regional recessions and of decades of financial instability on the parts of businesses and individuals who had no other providers of financial intermediation services close enough to their homes.

The problems associated with wild cat banks and the pressures of sustaining the federal effort during the Civil War led Congress to create a national paper currency and national banks in the 1860's.[3] Eventually, the need for financial stability, including stable prices, and sound monetary policy was so great as to cause Congress to establish the Federal Reserve System. Federal authority in this arena has remained in place since that time – through various "gold standard" debates, the creation of the Bretton Woods' Agreement that established the current international monetary systems in the 1940's, and to the present. The federal government has the sole power to issue "legal tender."[4]

All of our principal trading partners also operate in national systems in which a single, state-specified currency constitutes "legal tender" for all transactions. There is little literature on the attitudes of our principal trading partners about "virtual currencies" – with the exception of coverage of Canada's development and plan to issue as "legal tender" forms of "digital currencies known as "MintChips,"[5] and the European Central Bank's 2012 report on *Virtual Currency Schemes*.[6] Canada's "Mint Chip" experiment reveals no intention of abandoning the principles set forth in *The Case of Mixed Money* in 1605: the prince, the stamp, and the value will continue to be the province of the sovereign. The ECB's report, as one would expect, also favors a continuing role for central banks and sovereign currencies.

But, just because "legal tender" exists as a fact in most developed nations, it does not follow that individuals or businesses cannot agree to take barter or non-legal tender in exchange for goods and services. It just dramatically increases some, primarily legal risks in those transactions, much as we saw with "wild cat" banking in the pre-Civil War period here, and in the disappearance of bitcoin exchanges in China and also the Czech Republic. In these cases, the risk of engaging in virtual currency transactions currently falls entirely on users.

We must recognize that some individuals and, apparently, an increasing number of businesses, see value in using forms of "virtual currencies" to complete their own transactions.[7] Can we prevent them from doing so? Probably not. Should the United States step up their regulatory efforts in this arena? My answer is not yet, and not until such time as stronger evidence suggests problems exist with these currencies that contribute to financial instabilities, or otherwise enable issuers or intermediaries to commit fraud on users or complicate monetary or other important public policies.

PART III. DISCUSSION OF RECOMMENDATIONS

> Recommendation 1: Retain the current division of regulation between the States and Federal Government – with prudential regulation of the non-depository providers of new payments systems with the States and retaining the anti-moneylaundering, anti-terrorism and economic sanctions regulations with the Federal Government.

The current balance between State and federal regulation affords more opportunities to follow developments in this area with lots of eyes on these innovations, ensure AML and economic sanctions goals are met, and allow room for innovation of these intriguing technologies that a comprehensive federal licensure and supervision scheme might not allow as well. Furthermore, having prudential regulation should contribute to the confidence among users – whether consumers or businesses – that their stored value is safe and that their transactions will be executed as expected.

The split between prudential money transmission regulation by the States, and anti-money laundering and economic sanctions/ anti-terrorism regulations by the Department of the Treasury reflects a robust regulatory, supervision and examination scheme for virtual currency transactions with much room on the prudential side of State regulation to promote product innovation without sacrificing important protections for users or, on the federal side, anti-money laundering (AML) or economic sanctions goals.

Some advocate for a single, federal scheme of licensure and regulation of virtual currencies and their providers. The proponents of this view should be careful what they wish for: they could find themselves unable to qualify for a federal license as the efforts of certain retailers to obtain approval from the Federal Deposit Insurance Corporation for their industrial loan operations (even after they had obtained a state ILC charter) or national bank or federal savings and loan charters. These federal approvals are also expensive and time-consuming processes with considerable discretion left to regulators to reject applicants. It is not clear to me that early applicants will enjoy the relief from 50- state regulation that they seem to expect.

Some individuals will not adopt payment methods they do not understand and whose rules of the road are not transparent. Thus, we should appreciate the longstanding role the States have played in *innovating regulations that have encouraged users to adopt new payments methods*. The work of the Uniform Law Commissioners and American Law Institute, begun more than 65 years ago, created the uniform and predictable provisions of the Uniform Commercial Code (UCC) that State Legislatures enacted. The UCC's predominance in payments regulation is now complemented by payments systems rules and bilateral agreements, including those that govern transactions that the UCC does not address, as well as limited federal laws and regulations. Federal regulations also may prompt faster user adoptions of new technologies, as many believe the Fair Credit Billing Act (FCBA) and the Electronic Fund Transfers Act (EFTA) did in the late 1960's and 1970's, respectively, even though the EFTA has been criticized for chilling certain ATM developments.

> Recommendation 2: Make providers of virtual currencies comply with the customer-identification program and AML compliance program requirements of Sections 326 and 352 of the USA PATRIOT Act, and with the economic sanctions regulations enforced by OFAC, just as other payments systems providers do. Virtual currency customers will have to reveal their identities to issuers or transaction intermediaries of the currencies they use. They should get the same federal financial privacy rights that users of other payments products have under the Right to

Financial Privacy Act of 1978 and Title V of the GrammLeach-Bliley Act.

My concern is that disintermediation of payments – the separation of payment flows from the comprehensive record-keeping and retention requirements applicable to payments that eventually flow through the banking system – makes it more difficult to determine the identities of senders and recipients of payments. This may contribute to the efficacy of the "layering" stage of money laundering, the passage of the funds or credits through so many hands that the identities of payments participants is obscured. This is an important concern for anti-money-laundering, anti-terrorism, anti-proliferation, and anti-tax-avoidance purposes.

> Recommendation 3: Encourage FinCEN to clarify the manner in which customer-identification and AML compliance requirements apply to virtual currencies to a greater degree if that is needed to stop banks from discontinuing their business relationships with virtual currency providers and other payments innovators. If banks cannot determine how to comply with FinCEN regulations, for example, they will cut off payments innovators before the innovators can attract investors and users to make it to the second-stage distributed computing and database technologies their current work may generate.

Depository institutions deserve the clearest guidance on how customer-identification and AML compliance requirements apply to virtual currencies. This is one of the few ways in which we can stop the recent spate of terminations of banking relationships with providers of virtual currencies – colloquially called "bank discontinuance."

Without the clearest possible guidance available for banks and investors, we are likely to experience a domestic decline in innovations and the potential loss of development of future associated uses of the distributed computing and database technologies such as for tracking tangible goods transactions or even in tracking and trading intangibles such as electronic mortgages and other evidences of equity or debt. Moreover, if bitcoins or other virtual currencies prove to garner even more widespread international adoptions, the United States will want to have a share of the productive research and applications capacity in the United States and may regret actions that send it offshore. [8] This would be even more important if distributed technologies developing in the next five years that would not suffer the perceived disadvantages of bitcoins today were to emerge.

On the other hand, we should not condone the virtual currency systems that market the anonymity of their users or claim immunity from otherwise applicable compliance responsibilities in the name of "innovation." If proponents of virtual currencies want access to profits for transactions in the United States, they should be prepared to comply with applicable laws, and, in specific, they should obtain sufficient information from customers to enable them to respond to properly authorized requests for access from federal or state regulators and law enforcement agencies.

A corollary of this recommendation involves providing financial privacy rights to users of virtual payments systems equal to those provided to users of more traditional payment systems. In the United States, two functionally different, federal financial privacy statutes should govern virtual currency transactions – the Right to Financial Privacy Act of 1978, which governs access to account and transaction information of individuals and businesses by the federal government, and Title V (Privacy) of the Gramm-Leach-Bliley Financial Services Act of 1999, which governs how providers of consumer financial products and services may use and share the non-public, personally identifiable information they hold, including with their functional or prudential regulators and with federal, state, and local law enforcement agencies. It is unclear that participants in virtual currency systems are enjoying these rights today. As banks increasingly buy providers of digital currencies to develop their own products, it is even clearer that customers should enjoy the same financial privacy protections, including due process rights, however limited they may be with border seizures and other Title 18 forfeiture provisions.

> Recommendation 4: Encourage payments systems innovators to adopt and publicize payment systems rules for their own systems and even to compete for customers on the basis of the system rules they adopt.

Whenever a consumer or business prepares to make or receive a payment it will want to have certainty that:

- the payment is authorized by the person from whose funds or credits the payment will be made,
- the person has sufficient funds or credits for the payment processor to deliver those funds on time to the payee/ recipient so that the payee/

recipient will receive "goods funds" instantly or in a reasonable period of time,

- the payment is made to the proper payee and in the time frame specified or expected by the person whose funds or credits are being used or consistently with any applicable contract between the obligor and payee,
- the payment, from the obligee's perspective, will become final at a specified time or after a specified interval and, from the obligor's perspective, that it will discharge the underlying obligation to pay for goods or services or to retire a debt.
- the payment has integrity – that is, the named payee/ recipient has not been altered, the amount has not been lowered or raised, or the funds will not be held up unreasonably in transit.

These are "regulatory" or system rule qualities that will allow the provider to maintain users' trust.

Additionally, every person or business that stores funds or other value with a bank or broker – or in this case with the issuer, exchange or other provider/ participant in a virtual currency transaction – wants suitable assurances that they can redeem/ retrieve their funds or value when they want to do so. This issue surfaced with bitcoins when the federal government froze some bank accounts belonging to the Mt. Gox Exchange and the Exchange was unable to pay holders of bitcoins when they sought to redeem value stored in bitcoins. Other issues related to value storage include whether any form of insurance against the insolvency of the issuer or exchange is available to protect those who deposit value or otherwise hold accounts that they have reasonable expectations to redeem on little or no notice, or even on predictable terms.

Some virtual currencies have attracted negative publicity, including recent publicity about the disappearance of a Bitcoin exchange based in China with $4.1 million of value that belonged to others. This type of negative publicity stands in the way of broader adoption of virtual currencies.

Prudential regulation and transparent system operating rules should help legitimate businesses offering virtual currencies attract more customers – assuming we have no reason today to fear competition for legal tender from current-day virtual currencies.

I encourage virtual currency issuers to create *payment systems rules* for their own systems and harbor some hope that issuers will compete to offer system rules that match the needs of the individuals and businesses who participate. Payment systems rules often precede full government regulations by long periods of time. Examples include traveler's cheques and bank wire transfers, and more recently automated clearing house transactions governed by the National Automated Clearing House Association and electronic checking processing systems that use ECCHO Operating Rules. New payments methodologies regulated too soon often do not receive the same levels of innovations. The primary example I can cite was based on a report by the Board of Governors of the Federal Reserve System following the enactment and implementation of the Electronic Fund Transfers Act in the late 1970's. The alternative to provider-created system rules may be more government regulation. This gives providers a choice between self-regulation for these specific customer protection purposes or more government regulation. I imagine they will give self-regulation careful consideration.

Payments systems that have not established transparent and uniform system rules normally suffer a worse fate: so few individuals or businesses will use them that they wither for lack of investors and of income. This happened to some extent in the United States to early offerors of "electronic money," including Mondex and Digicash, despite talented senior management and significant investments. Consumers did not adopt them so merchants did not adopt them – in part because neither group was certain of their rights if they adopted them.

> Recommendation 5: Ignore the claims that any regulation of virtual currencies will halt innovations or that innovators deserve freedom from regulations that apply to other payments systems and their providers, and their wishes for a single federal licensure system.

I urge Members to resist the "we're new so don't regulate us at all" arguments that you've heard since the advent of electronic commerce. Payments are payments and stored value is value storage. The "don't regulate us or you will stifle innovation" arguments did not persuade many as digital money, prepaid cards, payroll cards and other new products appeared in markets and they offer no reason to abandon existing prudential regulation now.

There also is no reason to reward "innovators" with freedom from regulations with which their "real world" competitors must comply. That would provide anti-competitive advantages to certain new entrants for which no justification appears.

> Recommendation 6: Monitor the development of virtual currency providers in case they transform their products into commodities or securities and, if this happens, then decide whether regulating their products under the applicable regulations makes more sense.

Bitcoins' values have been highly volatile over the past year. This volatility looks like price volatility associated with commodities and securities; bitcoin prices seemingly move separately from the values of the world's major currencies. If other virtual currencies demonstrate this market freedom from legal tender currencies, this may be the signal that a reconsideration of type of regulation to be applied from regulation as payment systems to regulation as commodities or securities.

> Recommendation 7: Leave room for non-depository and depository providers of payments products to innovate in the virtual currency space.

It is important not to rush new laws or regulations following negative publicity from a new technology when existing laws regulate issuers prudentially and clarity in enforcement of AML regulations can allow some space for innovators in the virtual currency space. I was delighted to read last week that the New York State Department of Financial Services was considering offering a BitLicense. Careful development of licensure standards will help develop stable payments products. As I have mentioned, virtual currency technologies can produce secondary, distributed computing and database applications that could yield enormous benefits to domestic and cross-border commerce.

> Recommendation 8: Ask for a study of virtual currencies to be carried out by the Federal Reserve Board or the Department of the Treasury or fund a study pursuant to the Federal Advisory Committees Act by an inter-agency task force and industry participants.

The subcommittees sponsoring today's hearing should ask for a study by the Board of Governors of the Federal Reserve System or the Department of the Treasury of virtual currencies, the potential for innovations and efficiencies they may offer more broadly, and the kinds of risks – to price stability, financial stability, payment system stability, reputational risks and for users – identified in an October 2012 report by the European Central Bank entitled "Virtual Currency Schemes."[9]

Another option is for Congress to authorize and separately fund an inter-agency working group to produce a study of how the various federal agencies involved in payments, regulating of banking, commodities, securities and law enforcement.

Regardless of which agency leads the study, the work should be organized under the Federal Advisory Committees Act so that all industry segments can be included.

PART IV. RESPONSES TO OTHER QUESTIONS POSED BY THE COMMITTEE

A. Issues Implicated In Cross-Border Payments and Cross-Border Trade and Finance

Monetary policy is one of the concerns cited by the European Central Bank in its 2012 report on Virtual Currency Schemes. But that report did not discuss enforcement of collateralized debt obligations.

Virtual currency transactions could render finance transactions non-transparent so that current and potential providers of financing might not be able to ascertain their relative priorities to assets that underlie those trade transactions. The United States will want to follow closely developments that frustrate creditors' claims to inventory or other assets if the obligor fails to complete payments for goods that it has purchased here or abroad. The trend away from bank-issued letters of credit to supply-chain financing not involving banks – indeed including financing provided by logistics suppliers – has not yet degraded the ability of sellers, buyers or their financers to monitor cross-border trade transactions. This may be because logistics suppliers of supply-chain finance enjoy hard-earned reputations as honest participants delivering the goods they carry and collecting payments if required on behalf of senders. But the potential for trade finance disruption still exists.

B. Possible Regulatory Models for Providers of Payments Products and Systems

In addition to the current state prudential regulation of virtual currency providers and to Treasury's comprehensive registration, AML and economic sanctions regulations applicable to money services businesses, we have a number of potential models for regulating, requiring registration or supervising and examining providers of virtual currencies. I mention these more for future purposes than for any need I perceive at this point, but the eventual use of alternative regulatory models depends in large measure on how the products offered as "virtual currencies" work in fact.

For example, state prudential regulation of money transmitters is framed to ensure that competent transaction execution. Those who take funds from one person with a promise to deliver them to a second person need to have the capacity to do just what they promise – to pay in the manner, in the time, and to the person that the first person instructed them to pay.

Prudential regulation by states establishes qualifications for providers – depository and non-depository providers they license to do business with their own residents, and establishes a system of reserves or bonds or both so that funds will be available to complete transactions on those persons' parts. [10] State licensing and bonding requirements are cited by many entrepreneurs as a reason why virtual currencies are not attracting the widespread uses and investor funding that entrepreneurs seek. However, without these state requirements, the prospect of value disappearing – as it apparently has with the disappearance of the bitcoin exchange in China – likely would rise and injure users of these products.

State prudential regulation began in the late 18th Century when Massachusetts and New Hampshire prohibited unincorporated banks from operating.[11] New York State followed them with its prohibition in 1804. Some states banned banking – period. These included Texas until 1904, and Iowa, Arkansas, Oregon and California before the Civil War. State laws also established "safety deposit" systems and have regulated them. Items in safety deposit boxes are not immune from asset freeze orders issued by courts, or seizure by the IRS. States have been regulating money transmitters since the advent of the telegraph.

The regulation of safe-storage systems is even more ancient, beginning with the Knights Templar and Vatican as lenders in the pre-and early Renaissance periods, and with the Silver Vaults in London and lenders in Belgium, the Netherlands, and Florence whose services contributed to the early Renaissance flows of commerce and modern trade. I mention safety deposit systems because of the similarities they have, and that their predecessors had, to products such as e-Gold, and even bitcoins. Some of these contemporary products are more like commodities to be bartered than they are true "currencies." [12]

Alternative regulatory schemes for virtual currencies include commodities and securities regulation. The securities model offers advantages such as registration and requirements for disclosing material events that may affect the value of the security or the health of its issuer.

One reason to consider commodities or securities regulatory schemes for virtual currencies that do not track the movements of legal tender currencies is evidence that investors are speculating in these currencies. To the extent that virtual currencies seem to be used more for speculative purposes and less for transaction execution, the non-payments models of regulations present feasible alternatives.

CONCLUSION

I applaud the Subcommittees for holding this important hearing and urge them to continue to watch developments in virtual currencies. Thank you again, Chairman Merkley and Chairman Warner, and Ranking Members Heller and Kirk, for this opportunity to share my views with your Subcommittees. I will be pleased to take questions.

End Notes

[1] The Case of Mixed Money in Ireland, Trin. 2 James I. AD 1605 [Davies' Reports]. A key sentence from the opinion in that case proclaimed: "that it appertaineth only to the King of England, to make or coin money within his dominions. [2 Ro. ab. 166. 1 Co. 146, 5 Co. 114. 1 H.H.P.C. 188.]" The court also announced its conviction that there were three attributes of "money" and "legal tender" that distinguished them: the price, the stamp, and the value. Id.

[2] See Marine Bank v. Fulton Bank, 69 U.S. (2 Wall.) 252 (1864) (upholding the depositor's right to the sum owed on bank notes by its bank, rather than the lower value prevailing for Illinois notes of the time, which had decreased by 50% in value during the year that collection took). "Wildcat banks" did not have reserves sufficient to back their issues. Lissa L. Broome & Jerry W. Markham, REGULATION OF BANK FINANCIAL SERVICE ACTIVITIES 17 (Thomson Reuters, 2011).

[3] The Stamp Payments Act of 1862, 12 Stat. 592; Rev. Stat. 711, sect. 3583 (prohibiting circulation of bank notes worth less than one dollar); National Currency Act of 1863, ch. 58, 12 Stat. 665 (Feb. 25, 1863) (authorizing the chartering of national banks); and the National Bank Act of 1864, act June 3, 1864, ch. 106, 13 Stat. 99, as amended (superceding the National Currency Act). The goal of these collective National Banking Acts

... was to create a uniform national currency. Rather than have several hundred, or several thousand, forms of currency circulating in the states, conducting transactions could be greatly simplified if there were a uniform currency. To achieve this all national banks were required to accept at par the banknotes of other national banks. This insured that national banknotes would not suffer from the same discounting problem with which state banknotes were afflicted. In addition, all national banknotes were printed by the Comptroller of the Currency on behalf of the national banks to guarantee standardization in appearance and quality. This reduced the possibility of counterfeiting, an understandable wartime concern. American History from Revolution to Reconstruction and Beyond, http://www.let.rug.nl/usa/essays/general/a-brief-history-of-central-banking/national-banking-acts-of-1863- and-1864.php (last visited Nov. 17, 2013). Problems of counterfeit or altered notes caused the creation of John Thompson's Bank Note Detector, a precursor of the listing of counterfeit and altered notes issued routinely by the Office of the Comptroller of the Currency and Federal Deposit Insurance Corporation today. The national currency was commodity currency backed by specie (e.g., gold certificates) in place of "greenbacks." Eventually, as the Members know, the United States replaced commodity currency with fiat currency in the form of Federal Reserve Notes. Proponents of virtual currencies and other followers of the Austrian School of Economics distrust fiat currencies for their roles in business cycles and consequences of monetary interventions reasons as explained well in the European Central Bank's 2012 report on Virtual Currency Schemes, virtualcurrencyschemes201210en.pdf, at 21. The Austrian School economists also prefer the "de-nationalization" of currency, effectively an end to governments' monopoly on the issuance of money. Id. These economists criticize fractional-reserve banking systems like ours, and urge the re-adoption of the gold standard. Id. Broome & Markham also note that as "electronic money" came into the market in the 1990's, commentators considered The Stamp Payments Act to bar its issuance in the nation. Supra, note 1 at 19.

[4] Congress' authority was upheld in a series of decisions including United States v. Van Auken, 96 U.S. (6 Otto) 366 (1977); Legal Tender Cases, Know v. Lee & Parker v. Davis, 79 U.S. (12 Wall.) 457 (1870); Veazie Bank v. Fenno, 75 U.S. (8 Wall.) 533 (1869). The federal government's authority thus preempts the issuance by states such as Virginia of competing currencies, as the Virginia Legislature proposed to do in the past year.

[5] Canada's plans have revolved around a state-created digital "currency" that they call "Mint Chips." For more information on the status of this development, see John Greenwood, Canadian Mint ready to test its own digital money project, FIN. POST (Canada) (Sept. 19. 2013).

[6] Available at virtualcurrencyschemes201210en.pdf (last visited Nov. 17, 2013). (The ISBN for this report is 9778-92-899-0862-7 (online).)

[7] Media reports cite reasons such as avoiding the expense of exchange of currencies and other transaction costs associated with use of debit or credit cards, or even checks.

[8] For a valuable discussion of the regulation of virtual currencies from the perspective of the European Central Bank, see Virtual Currency Schemes, supra note 6. This study does not accurately reflect the current state of regulation of virtual currencies in the United States in two respects. First, it ignores the presence of state prudential regulation of "money transmitters." Also, it fails to reflect the fact that widely used payments systems here have already moved away from reliance on "payments laws" and towards system rules and bilateral agreements for processing payments. These system rules and bilateral agreements often augment laws that otherwise apply to the underlying form of payment being used, but in other cases they provide uniformity and certainty to forms of payments that neither federal or state laws comprehensively govern (credit cards, electronic fund transfers, and certain aspects of payroll cards, for example). The Bank's report mentions a case in which

French "banks shut down the currency exchange facility for accounts handling [bitcoins], on the presumption that Bitcoin should conform to electronic money regulations. Id. at 43, citing Finextra:http://www.finextra.comnews.fullstory.aspx?newscemid=22921.

[9] Supra, note 6. For more information about this report, see supra, note 8.

[10] This system has features of fractional reserves that our banking system depends on, as well as of bonding or comparable requirements to ensure completion of transactions in the event of provider failure. The Board of Governors of the Federal Reserve System also establishes reserve requirements for depository institutions on an annual basis, in Regulation D.

[11] For a brief discussion of this period in bank and payments regulation in the United States, see Broome & Markham, supra, note 2 at 1-28.

[12] Francois R. Velde, Bitcoin: A primer, CHIC. FED LETTER No. 317 (Dec. 2013) (copy on file with the witness) (describes the operations of bitcoins and, particularly, its unique methods for controlling two challenges of digital money – controlling the creation and avoiding duplication of units).

In: Virtual Currency …
Editor: Valerie Duskin

ISBN: 978-1-63117-280-9

Chapter 12

STATEMENT OF PAUL SMOCHER, BITS PRESIDENT, FINANCIAL SERVICES ROUNDTABLE. HEARING ON "THE PRESENT AND FUTURE IMPACT OF VIRTUAL CURRENCY"*

Thank you Chairmen Warner and Merkley, Ranking Members Kirk and Heller and Members of the Committee for the opportunity to testify before you today.

My name is Paul Smocer and I am the President of BITS, the technology policy division of The Financial Services Roundtable. BITS addresses issues at the intersection of financial services, technology and public policy, on behalf of its one hundred member institutions, their millions of customers, and all of the stakeholders in the US financial system.

The financial services market constantly evolves and matures to reflect the explosive growth of technological capacity, entrepreneurial innovation and consumer needs and preferences. The topic of today's hearing, "Virtual Currency," has been and continues to be an area of focus for our member companies and within the industry. As virtual or digital currencies have evolved, our members discuss the potential benefits as well as potential drawbacks – particularly drawbacks related to security, fraud and consumer

* This is an edited, reformatted and augmented version of a statement, presented November 19, 2013 before the Senate Committee on Banking, Housing, and Urban Affairs, Subcommittee on National Security and International Trade and Finance.

impact. My testimony today will cover the evolution of digital currency, as well as opportunities and risks.

DIGITAL CURRENCY EVOLUTION

Since the commercialization of the Internet, the concept of digital money has held intrigue. The terms "virtual currencies" and "digital currencies" are the generally accepted vernacular terminology used to identify forms of electronic currency that can be used to effect transactions involving true goods and services.

Attempts to develop digital currencies, and the methodologies used to exchange them for value, have existed for several decades. For example, in the 1990s, we saw attempts such as NatWest's Mondex card, which was an attempt at creating an electronic cash card that acted as alternative to coins and banknotes, and DigiCash Inc., which was an electronic money corporation founded by David Chaum. The regulatory community has also been thinking about this subject for some time. For example, in September 1996, the United States Department of the Treasury held a conference entitled "Toward Electronic Money and Banking: The Role of Government" that explored this issue. Until recently, however, attempts to launch digital currencies have been unsuccessful. What makes today's environment different and enhances the probability of success in launching digital currencies? The answers to that question include:

- Consumers are much more comfortable in transacting online through traditional financial systems as well as other vehicles such as online games that leads consumers to an increasing overall comfort with the online world.
- Computer systems are more powerful and less expensive thus facilitating some of the processing intensive techniques associated with emergent digital currencies.
- A growing interest in having an international currency free of some of the factors such as exchange rate considerations, inter-currency transactional fees, etc.
- The increasing desire for privacy.
- The general cache that some attach to the concept and to innovative developments on the Internet.

- And sadly, but realistically, a desire to facilitate illegal activities such as money laundering, fraud, and terrorism financing.

This has allowed a market for, though still on a limited basis, digital currency and the development of some infrastructures to support the exchange of digital currency.

Bitcoin is often the focus of digital currency discussions as it is the largest independent digital currency. Bitcoins are created through a digital process, "mining", which involves computer programs working on the same set of data to solve a puzzle. Across the Internet, a Bitcoin is mined every 10 minutes through this process with allegedly a maximum of 21 million allowed in circulation. Once mined, the owner is able to use his or her Bitcoins at any participating merchant and the transactions are tracked through a public ledger known as a block chain, which identifies users by a unique code. Bitcoin users review these ledgers to validate transactions and to ensure that users are spending existing Bitcoins. These transactions operate outside of the traditional payments system. Thus, they would not intersect with credit card, ACH or other trusted financial services networks. The system is not run by any one entity or company, but rather is supported by participants in the Bitcoin environment.

Unlike depository accounts held in traditional financial institutions, Bitcoin ownership is not associated with any named individuals. Owners of individual accounts are recognized by unique codes intended to assure their anonymity. Even the creator of Bitcoin is considered anonymous. Its creation is often attributed to a Satoshi Nakamoto, though it is speculated that this is actually a pseudonym for an anonymous individual or group of anonymous web developers. In general, Bitcoin provides a decentralized system, using peer-to-peer networking, digital signatures and cryptographic proofing to enable funds transfers between participants.

Other entities in the digital marketplace, such as Ripple, rely on the efficiencies of the Internet by developing an open source digital transaction protocol. Ripple uses existing currencies or valuable items (e.g., airline miles), which are converted into its internal currency called XRP. Users can then quickly transact within XRP. Individuals can convert funds back to a monetary value by selling the XRP. Similar to Bitcoin, Ripple includes an open ledger to allow all participants to see the activity of the system and validate transactions, again with individual accounts recognized by a unique code. These transactions also would not cross the traditional payments, but could leverage the existing funds in a financial institution consumer's account as an individual could directly transfer dollars into their Ripple account. A unique feature of Ripple is to allow individuals to provide loans to others within the network. Individuals establish their own ability to trust different users and decide how much they would like to loan the individual. In addition, a trust score can be assessed to different users.

OPPORTUNITIES

As we think about the opportunities associated with digital currencies, I believe we need to think of them in two distinct areas – the concept of the currency itself and the infrastructure mechanisms being created to exchange them.

We have witnessed the concepts of new, emerging currencies before. Some have noted that even within our country, the creation of new currencies was an early part of our history as the states, regions, and even merchant exchanges established currencies. What makes digital currencies different is that they allow the concept of cash or a cash equivalent to be used over the Internet. That fact, in turn, essentially makes them a global form of currency.

One measure of a currency's success is its acceptability. An emergent trend is that institutions such as international and large retailers are beginning to accept select digital currencies as payment for goods and services. For example, in November 2012, the web publishing service WordPress announced they would accept Bitcoin as a form of payment for WordPress upgrades. Interestingly too, just last week, we all became aware that the Federal Election Commission is seriously considering letting candidates and committees accept Bitcoins as in-kind contributions. Given digital currencies today rely neither on government-sponsored central banks nor have the backing of any national currency, merchant acceptance and certainly acceptance by government agencies tends to help these currencies establish their legitimacy and increase the trust parties have in them and their stability in the marketplace. At this point, however, the established financial services industry still does not generally recognize these currencies as broadly accepted.

One important aspect to recognize is that, as digital currencies become more internationally accepted, there is a growing recognition of their ability to increase international sales opportunities and their ability to facilitate simpler international funds transfers. Returning to the WordPress example of retailer acceptance, WordPress found the acceptance of digital currencies allowed it access to new consumers in countries where traditional payment systems do not permit access for financial, security or international sanction reasons.

Because of the ability to work internationally and outside of existing markets, some suggest digital currencies also have the ability to provide affordable access to the unbanked on a global scale. For example, a mobile phone based money transfer and microfinancing service in Kenya backed by Kenya's largest two mobile network operators called M-Pesa, recently added a Bitcoin payment option for customers in Kenya.

In addition, digital currencies can assist individuals in countries with repressive regimes to support causes or efforts that they might otherwise not be able to support. For example, in certain countries where citizens fall under strict government control, individuals can often not donate to or purchase from sites that are banned by their country's traditional payments providers. These transactions are made easier using decentralized, unaffiliated, anonymous currencies with their own payment infrastructures. Because of this, often times digital currencies are referred to as a "censorship-resistant" currency.

If digital currencies reach a state where their economic stability is more assured, they can also function as an outside currency that can provide additional economic security for individuals living in a country whose own currency is under financial distress. For example, during the recent Cyprus and Argentina financial crises, citizens transferred funds to digital currencies, mostly Bitcoin, to provide a more steady assurance for the security of their funds.

The infrastructure supporting digital currency payments has some appealing quality to merchants also due to the lack of interchange fees. For many, digital currencies can provide a lower transaction cost to the benefit of both merchants and consumers. Digital currencies may be more attractive to merchants as many do not allow the payments to be reversed, so there is no opportunity for chargebacks.

Another interesting aspect related to certain digital currencies is their cryptographic protections. Ostensibly, the cryptography is intended to provide a level of security that both helps limit the amount of a currency in circulation and to bolster their providers' claims that their currencies cannot be duplicated or counterfeited. The currency providers also claim that the financial information about any particular user's wallet (e.g., their identity, their balance) is anonymous and, therefore, more secure than in other Internet-based financial transaction environments. If these claims hold true, which is questionable, this could be very significant for the future of monetary security.

In summary then, digital currencies and their supporting infrastructure do indeed present opportunities that we are closely watching. They could provide a model for how to facilitate real-time payments – particularly those involving international parties and those involving micropayments. They offer some opportunity to explore deeper cryptographic options for Internet-based transactions and they may offer opportunities to serve more effectively the under-banked and those who are truly politically repressed.

RISKS

While the opportunities noted above have piqued the interest of the financial services industry in digital currencies, we also have to recognize a plethora of potential risks.

First, digital currencies pose significant market risk. Without government funding or support, digital currencies may be subject to extreme market volatility. The participants in the market itself have to decide the worth of each currency. Given the immaturity of the market, slight changes in the market can produce significant swings in value. In addition, the value of items purchased could change drastically and there would not be a single arbitrator to provide final decisions as to the value of the currency. Bitcoin is the best example of market volatility. Since its creation four years ago, the market has gone through several significant swings in value, including in 2011 when the value fell 90 percent from $30 to $3. Recently, its value took a steep dive again when the use of Bitcoins was associated with the alleged operations of the drug ring known as "Silk Road." While its value has bounced back, broad swings in value create significant risk to both holders of the currency and to merchants and others who accept the currency as payment. With an established currency, merchants can generally be assured that the payment they receive will be of equal value to the service or merchandise purchased. With a currency that can fluctuate wildly, there is significantly more risk and little to no recourse for the merchant if the payment currency's value falls significantly. If the transaction happens to be international, the payment settlement methods used with established currencies do not apply. If, for example, one makes a purchase with a credit card issued in the US from a UK-based merchant, the payment infrastructure will convert the purchase price from British pounds to US dollars at a market rate and post that amount to the purchaser's account. The infrastructure to support this type of conversion is only in its infancy with the digital currency world. As well, we simply do not yet have enough experience to know if these currencies will even continue to exist. Many factors including broader acceptability will influence whether we see an increase or collapse in value of these currencies.

On the consumer side, the use of these currencies and the infrastructure exchange mechanisms they utilize are currently subject to few of the consumer protections we have come to expect in the traditional world of currency and payments. In addition, since these currencies do not carry clear and effective disclosures, even the most sophisticated consumers are unlikely to be aware of and understand the risks associated with them.

At this point, in the US, the Financial Crimes Enforcement Network (FinCEN) has taken the regulatory lead by creating its formal statement on digital currencies. This March 2013 guidance clarified the responsibilities of participants in the digital currency marketplace to register as money services businesses and money transmitters. Given the decentralized approach of the currencies, this requires registration by many individuals who previously did not consider themselves part of this network. Beyond this March guidance of FinCEN, digital currency providers have virtually no existing regulatory oversight. This is even more meaningful for currency providers and users operating outside regulated countries. Without regulations, these digital currencies are not providing appropriate consumer protections to ensure individuals understand the risks much less are protected in ways we now take for granted. As examples:

- If the value in an individual's digital currency account is fraudulently stolen, the victim has no recourse to recover the funds. In fact, within the last two months there have been multiple reports of Bitcoin currency disappearances from various Bitcoin trading platforms. Some allegedly involved hacks into Bitcoin repositories. At least one allegedly involved the creation of an "unlicensed" repository into which Bitcoin owners deposited their funds only to have the repository suddenly disappear. In none of these cases is it expected that the owners will recover a single Bitcoin. Contrast that to the recourse available to a consumer who is a bank customer. If funds are fraudulently taken from the consumer's deposit account, the bank will make that customer whole. If an entire institution that is an FDIC-insured depository institution were to fail due to a major cyber-attack, consumers would generally be afforded protections that would allow them to recover a significant balance of their deposit accounts.

- If a consumer's digital currency account were used to make an unauthorized payment, laws that limit the amount of consumer financial responsibility and require investigation by the financial institution holding the consumer's transaction or credit card would not apply. The consumer would simply lose the value of the fraudulent payment.
- While there is an emerging trend in the regulatory community, led by FinCEN at the federal level, to consider the classification of certain parties in the digital currency world as money transmitters, laws and regulations that apply to funds transfers occurring through traditional financial institutions currently have little relevance in the digital currency world. There is no method for attrition or preemptively stopping the transfer of digital currency funds.

These types of fraud protections provided by the financial services industry have developed into an essential part of overall consumer protection. Without some level of parity, today's digital currency consumers are essentially unprotected.

It is important to note however, that while the digital currency market seems ripe for further oversight and regulation, the act of regulating it, in and of itself, adds legitimacy to the market.

Another risk related to digital currencies involves the fact that most digital currencies are stored in digital wallets that are associated with personal computers or devices. Once these devices are compromised, there are no additional ways for the consumer to access their funds. In addition to the fraud risks noted above, there have been several recent cases of hacks on digital wallets that hold digital currencies. These hacks use similar techniques to traditional hacking efforts we have seen in the financial services industry. For example, phishing techniques are used to gain access to a user's information needed for authentication.

It is important to recognize too that while FinCEN has taken some action and others at the federal and state levels are considering regulatory actions, currently none of the digital currency operators or infrastructure providers are subject to the intense level of regulatory oversight applied to regulated and chartered financial providers. They are not subject to any required regulatory standards regarding, for example, cyber security and data breach notification requirements that grew out of the Gramm Leach Bliley Act. They are not subject to the regulatory and best practices guidance issued by the Federal Financial Institutions Examination Council and its member agencies that they have developed over the last 20 years. Likewise, they are not subject to independent examination of their controls environments by any regulatory authority. Because digital currency transactions typically occur within privately operated, unregulated networks, financial and security risk determination and mitigation is left up to the currency or infrastructure provider.

In addition, while many digital currencies tout that they are anonymous, they rely on a unique identifier for each account. Through analysis of transactions or confirmation by an individual, these identifiers could be connected with an individual. Given that digital currencies rely on a public ledger, the individual's transaction could become knowledgeable to individuals who have been identified.

Earlier I noted in the "Opportunities" section the ability for individuals to provide funds to legitimate organizations that their native country might inappropriately ban. This can also work in the reverse. Using digital currencies, individuals may also be able to donate to illegal organizations that would otherwise be legitimately banned by one or more governments. The ability for governments to ban payments to sites, for example, is a useful technique in thwarting illegal activity and terrorist funding.

Allowing digital currencies, particularly ones that by design are intended to provide full anonymity to the currency holders, has also invited their use for illicit activities. In fact, some recent studies suggest that the anonymous nature of digital currencies has made them a haven for illegal activity. The most notable recent example is the FBI case that resulted in the take down of Silk Road – an operation that allegedly was used to anonymously buy or sell illegal drugs, offer guns and assassins for sale, and provide tutorials on hacking ATM machines. The operation was completely reliant on digital currency for transactions. When this site was taken down, law enforcement had numerous challenges in seizing the funds of the site and those of Silk Road's alleged operators and customers.

The digital currency environment is also being used as a new way to launder money. A recent major example would be the situation involving the May 2013 indictment of Liberty Reserve. Liberty Reserve was a global currency exchange that allegedly ran a $6 billion money-laundering operation online ostensibly serving as an exchange for criminals engaged in various illegal activities. According to the prosecutors who presented the charges, Liberty Reserve was responsible for laundering billions of dollars, conducting 55 million transactions that involved millions of customers around the world, including about 200,000 in the United States. It is also important to note that all a user need to do to use the system was to provide a name, address and date of birth. However, unlike the Know Your Customer requirements that apply to traditional financial institutions, Liberty Reserve, being unregulated and incorporated outside the US, was not required to validate customers' identities. As the indictment stated, "Accounts could therefore be opened easily using fictitious or anonymous identities."

While the Silk Road and Liberty Reserve situations serve as examples, the point here is that digital currencies are being used to assist a broad array of criminal activities including illegal drug sales, stolen identities, child pornography, prostitution, human trafficking, and illegal weapons sales. It is also being used as a favorite of cyber criminals to pay for services such as developing and distributing malicious software to the movement of stolen funds resulting from account take overs.

One additional consideration is the level of clarity that currently exists regarding how virtual currencies will be treated within the tax code and whether virtual currencies offer an ability to evade taxes. In May 2013, the United States Government Accountability Office issued a report to the US Senate's Committee on Finance entitled, "Virtual Economies and Currencies, Additional IRS Guidance Could Reduce Tax Compliance Risks." The report suggests that the IRS should determine and subsequently address the need for additional tax guidance and additional taxpayer education.

The lack of regulatory oversight, the risks to consumers and the market risks associated with digital currency provide a continuing challenge to its overall legitimacy, usage and endorsement by the financial services industry.

Conclusion

In conclusion, there is no denying that the use of digital currencies will continue to evolve. Consequently, we will continue to discuss that growth and the associated opportunities and risks. As with the Internet and electronic commerce in general, we have seen innovations grow from early concepts where the risks outweighed the advantages to, over time, becoming an accepted norm. For now, I would opine we are not yet there with digital currencies. They do provide opportunities – or more accurately perhaps suggest areas of opportunity, but we will need to address the threats to consumers and society, the need for appropriate regulation and the effectiveness of risk mitigations. As the discussion continues, we would be happy to continue to participate, particularly where it would be advantaged by public-private collaborations such as through the Federal Reserve Banks study of the future of the payments system.

Thank you for your invitation to testify to the Subcommittees this afternoon. We look forward to continuing to work with you relative to this emerging technology.

In: Virtual Currency …
Editor: Valerie Duskin

ISBN: 978-1-63117-280-9

Chapter 13

TESTIMONY OF DAVID J. COTNEY, COMMISSIONER OF BANKS, MASSACHUSETTS DIVISION OF BANKS. HEARING ON "THE PRESENT AND FUTURE IMPACT OF VIRTUAL CURRENCY"*

INTRODUCTION

Good afternoon Chairmen Warner and Merkley, Ranking Members Kirk and Heller. My name is David Cotney and I serve as the Commissioner of Banks for the Commonwealth of Massachusetts. The Massachusetts Division of Banks is responsible for the overseeing all state-chartered banks and credit unions as well as regulating a range of non-bank financial service providers including money transmitters. I also serve as the Vice Chairman of the Board of Directors of the Conference of State Bank Supervisors (CSBS), and as the Chairman of the State Liaison Committee of the Federal Financial Institutions Examination Council (FFIEC).[1]

It is my pleasure to testify before you today on behalf of CSBS. CSBS is the nationwide organization of banking regulators from all 50 states, the District of Columbia, Guam, Puerto Rico, and the U.S. Virgin Islands. For more than a century, CSBS has given state supervisors a national forum to coordinate supervision and to develop regulatory policy. CSBS also provides

* Presented November 19, 2013 before the Senate Committee on Banking, Housing, and Urban Affairs, Subcommittee on National Security and International Trade and Finance.

training to state banking and financial regulators and represents its members before Congress and the federal financial regulatory agencies.

State banking regulators supervise over 5,200 state-chartered banks.[2] The majority of state banking departments also regulates a variety of non-bank financial services providers, including money services businesses (MSBs) as well as mortgage lenders, check cashers, and payday lenders. This broad supervisory portfolio provides state regulators with a unique perspective in the payments landscape. Unlike any single federal prudential regulator, most states regulate all of the financial intermediaries in the payments system: banks, credit unions, and money transmitters.

I thank you for holding this hearing on virtual currency. The risks virtual currency presents impact consumer protection, payment systems stability, money laundering, national security, and tax evasion. The potential benefits are similarly multi-faceted: speed and efficiency, lower transaction costs, and providing an outlet for the unbanked and underbanked around the world. To address these areas, state regulators view our responsibility as supervising in a manner that mitigates risks while not impeding industry innovation and flexibility.

States and state regulation have served as a forum for market experimentation as well as an early warning system of troublesome consumer and market trends. As the laboratories of innovation, the states welcome technology developments in the payments system that can lead to greater choice, security, and lower costs for consumers. Whether it's the Cambodian community in Lowell, the Somali community in Minneapolis, or the unbanked in Portland, Oregon, the states have a responsibility to ensure their citizens have the best possible options for transmitting value in a manner that does not put people, businesses, the payments system, or national security at risk.

My testimony today discusses existing state regulatory regimes and processes that offer the ability to supervise payment systems participants in a manner that promotes trust, confidence, and regulatory collaboration. I will also set out state regulators' efforts to further define priorities and approaches moving forward.

PAYMENT SYSTEMS AND STATE SUPERVISION

Payments systems are increasingly dynamic, signaling a shift in the way consumers and businesses pay for goods and services as well as the manner in which funds are remitted domestically and globally. Whether point of sale technologies, payment system intermediaries, or virtual currencies, development is ongoing and the possibilities are promising. However, while the opportunity for economic and consumer benefit is significant, so is the opportunity for real time losses and other destabilizing effects.

Nowhere are opportunities and challenges more starkly visible than in the emerging field of virtual currencies. Virtual currencies are decentralized digital mediums of exchange that, depending on the structure, serve as a hybrid of types of value. Today's virtual currencies are mostly math based, finite, verifiable, and open source, factors that present an opportunity to enhance the basic manner in which we conceive the exchange of value. In addition to virtual currencies, the business of transmitting value continues to evolve through mobile and web-based technologies that allow for instant and mobile payments on a secure basis.

To understand the opportunities and the risks presented in this sector, state agencies are actively monitoring new entrants into the digital market, including recent high-profile law enforcement actions related to virtual currency. State regulators are engaged in open discussions with a broad range of industry participants, joint state and federal working groups, and state-to-state coordination and strategic planning. States are also using their regulatory and legislative tools to learn more about the industry and increase transparency. For example, the New York Department of Financial Services launched an inquiry in August[3] and recently announced it will hold public hearings on virtual currency with an eye toward identifying possible licensing regimes.[4] New York's goal is one all states share, to determine appropriate regulatory guidelines that "allow new technologies and industries to flourish, while also working to ensure that consumers and our national security remain protected."[5] The California legislature has also worked to give regulators more tools to make the licensing process more transparent, authorizing the Department of Business Oversight to make written guidance public and offer guidance to prospective licensees.[6]

The states have a legal and regulatory structure that encompasses a broad range of financial services offered by a variety of bank and non-bank providers. For emerging payment technologies and alternative currencies, the threshold issue is the electronic movement of value owned by others – conduct over which the states have an existing structure for regulation and oversight. Money services businesses are entities that provide money transmission, currency exchange, prepaid access, monetary instruments as well as check cashing products and services. These companies provide a variety of financial products and services to a diverse customer base ranging from sophisticated financial customers to the underbanked and unbanked. One type of MSB, money transmitters, conducts remittance transfer services, domestically and internationally.

State MSB regulation recognizes the reality that money transmitters are local in touch, global in scale, and include a broad range of business models. A money transmitter's business platform may include telephone, online, authorized agent locations, or a combination thereof to reach its customer base. Additionally, a money transmitter may offer several different types of MSB activities simultaneously. For example, Moneygram Payment Systems – a company licensed in 48 states, the District of Columbia, and Puerto Rico – offers money transmission, bill payment, prepaid cards, and money orders through their online platform and authorized agents nationwide. As technology has evolved to include mobile payments and digital commerce, state money transmitter regulation has demonstrated the flexibility to supervise these products and services to consumers.

At the most basic level, many of the new products and services receive, hold, and send funds domestically or internationally. As such, these activities could fit into state money transmission definitions: the accepting or delivering of currency, funds, or other value, to another location or person by electronic means.[7]

CREDENTIALING OF FINANCIAL SERVICES PROVIDERS

Given the position of trust and confidence held by money transmitters and their critical function within local economies,[8] state law generally requires the licensing of companies and individuals that transmit other people's funds. By credentialing those who take and send monetary value on behalf of others, the states limit potential consumer harm and add stability to financial markets. In turn, licensed companies increase consumer and commercial confidence, which encourages the economic stability needed to support successful innovation.

Licensing communicates to the public that a licensee is viable, secure, and able to protect funds. State regulatory agencies license and regulate money transmitters to ensure compliance with state and federal regulatory requirements, to help prevent the use of money transmitters to finance illicit activities such as narcotics trafficking and terrorism, while also providing consumer protection for residents. Oversight includes ensuring the proper policies, procedures, and safeguards are in place to protect the company and its customers from operational, monetary, and fraud risk. Many states have utilized the Uniform Money Services Act, adopted by the National Commission on Uniform State Laws as the outline for their statutory provisions, which includes licensing standards, financial stability requirements, and regulatory principles.

Prospective licensees must file an application that typically includes the submission of credit reports, fingerprints, a business plan, financial statements, and a surety bond. The prospective licensee may provide evidence of policies, procedures, and internal controls that will facilitate the organization's compliance with state and federal regulations, including required Financial Crimes Enforcement Network (FinCEN) registration and documentation of a Bank Secrecy Act (BSA) compliance program.[9] Once a license is granted, management is required to maintain requisite permissible investments,[10] surety bonds, and submit periodic reports that often include financial statements, permissible investments calculations, branch and agent reporting, and transmission volume activity.

One of the main purposes of licensing is credentialing the entities and individuals seeking to engage in money transmission. Prospective licensees may be required to undergo rigorous requirements with the state agencies that include dialogue with the applicant regarding their business plan. The application may also include a background check on all owners, a requirement common in the MSB, banking, mortgage, securities, and other financial industries to ensure persons in a position of trust meet established standards to protect consumers and businesses alike. While some have complained that the process is cumbersome, most licensees recognize the value of identifying and validating market participants.

Credentialing requirements are vital and elementary to consumer protection. Some comments to date suggest this process is invasive and/or unnecessary, a view that reflects inexperience with time-validated requirements and unfamiliarity with the public policy goals served by licensing and regulatory oversight. We have seen this type of initial reaction as the states have enhanced their regulatory responsibilities, such as with the licensing of mortgage brokers and payday lenders. State legislatures have been very deliberate in crafting a credentialing process designed around the core objectives of consumer protection and promoting safety and soundness. State agencies would be negligent in their responsibilities if they simply allowed the push of technological innovation to preempt the need to apply the law in a thorough and deliberate manner.

SUPERVISION OF FINANCIAL SERVICES PROVIDERS

State agencies examine licensed money transmitters on a 12 to 24 month cycle to ensure licensees operate in a safe, sound, and legal manner. Between exams, state regulators monitor their licensees on an ongoing basis by reviewing the information submitted pursuant to reporting requirements. Licensees have periodic reporting requirements covering financial statements, permissible investments adequacy, branch and agent listings, and transmission volume activity. Consumer complaints provide another input into the supervisory process.

During the course of an examination, state examiners review complaints, capital, asset quality, management, earnings, operations, and compliance with the Bank Secrecy Act and the institution's anti-money laundering program. All these areas of review provide state agencies with data and other information to assess if a licensee is complying with applicable laws and conducting business in a safe and sound manner. If a licensee is found operating in an unsafe manner or out of compliance with state and federal requirements, the licensee may face state enforcement actions.

State enforcement actions vary depending on the entity, substantiated behavior, and violation. Importantly, enforcement is subject to appeal to an administrative hearing, ensuring licensees are afforded due process. For less serious findings warranting redress, the regulator and the regulated entity might agree to a letter of understanding or consent order, acknowledging the violation and setting forth a corrective plan. For more serious violations, temporary or permanent cease and desist orders will be issued, potentially limiting or even halting an entity's ability to operate. In more egregious circumstances, civil money penalties will be imposed in addition to any consumer restitution. Additionally, an entity's license could be revoked and the regulator's findings may necessitate referral to state and/or federal law enforcement.

STREAMLINED AND COORDINATED OVERSIGHT

Many state MSB licensees hold licenses in more than one state. Consequently, state agencies have proactively built a foundation for multi-state coordination and examinations. The Money Transmitters Regulators Association (MTRA)[11] formed the foundation for multi-state MSB efforts by executing the Money Transmitter Regulators Cooperative Agreement (MTRA Agreement) in 2002[12] and the MTRA Examination Protocol (MTRA Protocol) in 2010. These documents established the initial framework for states to coordinate MSB examinations and share information.

The MTRA Agreement started the states on the path to coordinated regulatory oversight by promoting concurrent and joint examinations among states. The MTRA Protocol provided a process for examinations, including multi-state examination schedules, work programs, and reports designed to increase effectiveness and reduce regulatory burden. Since the MTRA Agreement and Protocol were implemented, state agencies have conducted over 300 multi-state MSB examinations. Through coordination, regulatory oversight is applied in a uniform manner, a benefit that has been publicly noted by industry.[13]

To foster consistency, coordination, and communication, the states have collaborated on the enhanced CSBS/MTRA Nationwide Cooperative Agreement for MSB Supervision[14] and the Protocol for Performing Multi-State Examinations. The CSBS/MTRA Agreement and Protocol will supplement an effective and efficient regulatory framework for licensees by establishing the Multi-State MSB Examination Taskforce (MMET) to oversee joint examinations. Representing all states, the MMET has 10 members, currently comprised of state regulators from California, Florida, New York, North Carolina, Ohio, Pennsylvania, Texas, Virginia, Washington, and Wyoming. The MMET is working on developing an enhanced supervisory program tailored to multi-state licensees that fosters a process of consistency and coordination among state agencies.

In its first year, the MMET has improved the MSB examination work program and identified MSBs that meet the criteria for multi-state examinations.

As a result of established processes and lines of communication, state agencies promptly communicate to one another to reduce the possibility of consumer harm when enforcement is necessary across state lines. Over the last several years, the Massachusetts Division of Banks and our sister states have been active in ensuring that the monies that consumers transmit are received by the intended recipients. When companies fail to deliver, we are the only regulators out there to help consumers who may have lost their hard earned money. When we learn that someone has lost their funds, either through fraud or the financial instability of the company, the Division can act swiftly and in collaboration with our state regulatory counterparts.

State collaboration and coordination was evident earlier this year when it became clear to the Division that a money transmitter was possibly misappropriating customer funds. The money transmitter in question primarily remitted funds to Brazil with transfers in excess of $122 million originating from Massachusetts in 2012 alone. During an examination that involved coordination with the Brazilian Central Bank and two private Brazilian banks, it was determined that transaction records were falsified, evidencing an even broader pattern of illegal activity.

As a result, we promptly issued a Cease and Desist order[15] to stop this company from accepting and transmitting money from Massachusetts consumers and initiated a coordinated response across 37-states.[16] My agency communicated the enforcement action to our sister states, held multi-state calls, and worked with other state regulators to ensure remittance transfers were received and customers were assisted in a timely manner. All consumers who lost money have been made whole. This investigation is ongoing, but demonstrates that state regulators are prepared and capable of promptly acting on a national and international basis.

STATE- FEDERAL COORDINATION

Equally important as inter-state action is meaningful coordination with federal regulatory agencies. States recognize the importance of a larger regulatory fabric and integrated oversight for consumer protection and national security. In many areas of bank and non-bank regulation and supervision, the states have found that a more coordinated approach better serves both consumers and regulated entities.

The FFIEC has proved a valuable venue for coordination on processes between state regulators and federal financial regulators across a wide range of supervisory issues and processes. Through the State Liaison Committee to the FFIEC, the states collaborate with the FFIEC on the Bank Secrecy Act/Anti-Money Laundering Examination Manual, and participate as voting members of the FFIEC BSA/AML Working Group, an interagency effort to enhance coordination of BSA/AML training, guidance, and policy. The responsibilities of the working group include ensuring consistent agency approaches and collaborating on emerging issues.

The states have also entered into memorandums of understanding with FinCEN and the Internal Revenue Service (IRS) to coordinate BSA/AML supervision in the non-bank sector.[17] As such, state agencies provide information to FinCEN and the IRS on a quarterly and annual basis. This information may include the number of BSA examinations conducted, referrals of BSA violations, and state enforcement actions. Additionally, state agencies worked collaboratively with FinCEN and the IRS on the FinCEN/IRS Bank Secrecy Act/Anti-Money Laundering Examination Manual for MSBs that was issued in 2008. State agencies also have provided resources to develop and conduct training for state and IRS examiners nationwide on BSA compliance for MSBs.

The Dodd-Frank Wall Street Reform and Consumer Protection Act (Dodd-Frank) recognized the importance of a holistic approach to supervision. States bring a local point of view and a hands-on approach that complements the national priorities and perspective of federal regulators. In addition to existing state/federal cooperative frameworks, Dodd-Frank established new expectations for coordination, collaboration, and information sharing between the states and federal regulators, including with the Consumer Financial Protection Bureau (CFPB).[18] In 2011, the states entered into an Information Sharing Memorandum of Understanding with the CFPB (Information-Sharing MOU).[19] This was the first such MOU that the CFPB signed. Sixty-one state agencies and the six state regulatory associations[20] have signed the Information-Sharing MOU, which lays the foundation for information-sharing and supervision and enforcement cooperation between the CFPB and state regulators. Additionally, the state system is coordinating with the CFPB through CSBS on examiner training, examination technology and procedures, and complaint sharing.

Building on the foundation of the Information-Sharing MOU, on May 20, 2013, CSBS on behalf of the state regulators entered into the 2013 CFPB-State Supervisory Coordination Framework (Framework)[21] for the purposes of implementing a state-federal process for coordinated supervision. Under the Framework, the State Coordinating Committee (SCC)[22] – representing nearly 100 state regulatory agencies covering mortgage, MSBs, payday lending, consumer finance, student lending, debt collection, and others – is charged with coordinating examination and enforcement efforts directly with the CFPB. Through the SCC, the state system has the opportunity to influence and direct supervisory policy on a nationwide basis for non-depository industries including emerging and innovative players in the mobile, payments systems, and virtual currency markets.

NATIONWIDE MULTI-STATE LICENSING SYSTEM

State regulators have long understood that regulation needs to adapt alongside marketplace changes in order to capture the benefits and mitigate the risks of innovation. State regulators also understand that, in the modern economy, businesses and markets grow irrespective of geographic boundaries. Accordingly, the states recognized a need to be able to effectively and efficiently license mortgage companies and mortgage loan originators, to keep track of bad actors, and to provide responsible actors with greater efficiency and consistency in the licensing process. To achieve these goals, the states collectively developed and currently operate through CSBS the Nationwide Multi-State Licensing System and Registry (NMLS or System). After success in the mortgage licensing arena, states are currently using the System to license other regulated businesses, including all 12 license types issued by the Massachusetts Division of Banks.

Originally developed as a voluntary state system for mortgage licensing and then codified in the Secure and Fair Enforcement for Mortgage Licensing Act of 2008 (SAFE Act),[23] NMLS is a web-based system that allows state-licensed non-depository companies, branches, and individuals in the mortgage, consumer lending, money services businesses, and debt collection industries to apply for, amend, update, or renew a license online for all participating state agencies using a single set of uniform applications.

Last year, NMLS expanded functionality to include MSBs. Massachusetts is among 15 states currently using NMLS for MSB licensing, and 14 more are scheduled to come onto the system in the next year. The System enables licensees to manage their licenses in one location for multiple states, while states are able to track the number of unique companies and individuals, as well as the number of licenses they hold in each state. As a system of record for state regulatory authorities and a central point of access for licensing, NMLS brings greater uniformity and transparency to these non-depository financial services industries while maintaining and strengthening the ability of state regulators to monitor these industries.

Both industry and regulators see great advantages to NMLS. During last year's House hearing on money services businesses, industry representatives testified that widespread adoption of the system "would eliminate duplication of effort and opportunities for error" and "urge[d] any changes at the federal level to accommodate and encourage its further development."[24] To that end, I want to thank Senators Hagan and Toomey for taking the lead in sponsoring S. 947, which enhances the confidentiality and privilege already built into the

NMLS. I also want to thank the other members of the Committee – Senators Merkley, Manchin, Heitkamp, and Johanns – who have signed on as co-sponsors of S. 947. With the passage of S. 947, state regulators will have full confidence in the expanded use of NMLS, bringing greater efficiency to the regulatory process.

In addition to shared functionality between regulators and industry, NMLS provides transparency to consumers seeking information on regulated companies and individuals. NMLS Consumer Access (www.nmlsconsumeraccess.org) is a fully searchable public website that allows consumers to view information concerning companies, branches, and individuals holding state licenses in the NMLS. In 2012, the information available on the website was upgraded to include public state regulatory actions for state licensees. The website also enables consumers to connect directly to state agencies for the purpose of submitting a consumer complaint against a state licensed company.

As we continue to expand NMLS into other license types, regulators and industry alike will have the benefit of streamlined licensing requirements at a single source, and NMLS will be an important tool to provide understanding and responsiveness to companies that are local in touch but global in scale. Considering this, we continue to recommend to our colleagues at FinCEN and the CFPB that they use NMLS for any federal registration requirements.[25] State regulators and CSBS are ready to work with our federal counterparts to bring registration and licensing requirements under one shared structure, and NMLS already has the proven capabilities and widespread support for such a streamlined process.[26]

LOOKING FORWARD

State regulators are keenly aware that constantly emerging technologies have brought exciting and innovative products to the financial marketplace that consumers are utilizing on a daily basis. I and my fellow state banking commissioners recognize the need to understand these innovations. We also understand that there is a desire by many in the payments and technology industries for greater clarity for both state and federal regulatory requirements.

State regulators have structures, processes, and systems in place to bring clarity and consistency, while promoting consumer protection, safety and soundness, and national security goals. The states stand ready to work with our federal counterparts, as well as with representatives from industry and consumer groups, to seek opportunities for greater clarity and consistency, allow for innovation in the payments systems, and both exploit the benefits and minimize the risks of such innovations.

To address this changing landscape, CSBS is currently exploring policy processes for framing and considering issues facing regulators. These threshold issues include establishing the right characterization of virtual currency,[27] the consumer protection needs raised by instantly settled payments,[28] the resolution of conflicts between commercial entities in an instantaneous transfer system, and whether – and in what manner -- states should license entities involved with digital currency.[29] Our consideration of these and other issues will inform our efforts to preserve marketplace stability while supporting constructive innovation. The states will continue to work with this goal in mind, expanding on a framework that ensures safety and soundness, minimizes the use of digital currencies to fund illicit activities, and protects consumers and across a diverse landscape of companies and business models.

Local understanding, coordination between regulators, and collaboration with policy makers has provided the states a unique ability to actively regulate a broad range of financial products and services in an effective and timely manner. We look forward to working with Congress and our federal regulatory partners toward an integrated and collaborative approach to all innovative financial products and services, ensuring individuals and economies are well served.

End Notes

[1] Since 2006, state depository regulators have had a voting seat on the FFIEC, an interagency body empowered to prescribe uniform principles, standards, and report forms for financial institution examinations. The State Liaison Committee is made up of representatives of state bank, credit union and savings bank regulators and serves as the formal means for state input and representation on the FFIEC.

[2] Federal Deposit Insurance Corporation Statistics on Depository Institutions, Report Date June 30, 2013.

[3] Notice of Inquiry on Virtual Currencies, NYDFS (12 August 2013) *available at* http://www.dfs.ny.gov/about/press2013/memo1308121.pdf. Superintendent Lawsky explains: "The emergence of Bitcoin and other virtual currencies has presented a number of unique opportunities and challenges. Building innovative platforms for conducted commerce can help improve the depth and breadth of our nation's financial system. However, we have also seen instances where the cloak of anonymity provided by virtual currencies has helped support dangerous criminal activity, such as drug smuggling, money laundering, gun running, and child pornography."

[4] Notice of Intent to Hold Hearing on Virtual Currencies, Including Potential NYDFS Issuance of a 'BitLicense,' NYDFS (14 November 2013) *available at* http://www.dfs.ny.gov/about/press2013/virtual-currency-131114.pdf.

[5] Notice of Inquiry on Virtual Currencies, *supra*.

[6] California Assembly Bill No. 786, Money Transmissions (2013-2014). Effective January 1, 2014. *Available at* http://leginfo.legislature.ca.gov/faces/billNavClient.xhtml?bill id=201320140AB786.

[7] "'Money transmission' means . . . receiving money or monetary value for transmission . . . ." Alaska Stat. § 06.55.990; Arkansas A.C.A. § 23-55-102 (12) (A); Hawaii HRS § 489D-4; Iowa Code § 533C.102; Kansas K.S.A. § 9-508; La. R.S. 6:1032; Michigan MCLS § 487.1003; Miss. Code Ann. § 75-15-3; N.C. Gen. Stat. § 53-208.2; N.D. Cent. Code, § 13-09-02; S.D. Codified Laws § 51A-17-1; New Hampshire RSA 399-G:1; Tex. Finance Code § 151.301; Vermont 8 V.S.A. § 2500; Va. Code Ann. § 6.2-1900.

[8] See, e.g., The California Money Transmitter Act, Cal Fin Code § 2000 et seq. ("The [California] Legislature finds and declares all of the following: * * * (c) The failure of money transmission businesses to fulfill their obligations would cause loss to consumers, disrupt the payments mechanism in this state, undermine public confidence in financial institutions doing business in this state, and adversely affect the health, safety, and general welfare of persons in this state.").

[9] BSA compliance programs include policies, procedures, and internal controls to detect and deter money laundering and other illegal activity.

[10] Permissible investments are low risk, liquid assets such as cash and high rated investments required to be maintained in case an institution is unable to meet its commitments or fails. Permissible investments must be equal to the outstanding transmissions, payment instruments, or prepaid access values in the state or in all states.

[11] MTRA is a national non-profit organization dedicated to the efficient and effective regulation of the money transmission industry in the United States of America. The MTRA membership consists of state regulatory authorities in charge of regulating money transmitters and sellers of traveler's checks, money orders, drafts, and other money instruments.

[12] The MTRA Cooperative Agreement can be found at http://www.mtraweb.org/about/cooperative-agreement/.

[13] "Recent developments in money transmitter regulation have been positive for regulated entities, as examinations by multi-state regulator teams have blossomed." Ezra C. Levine, Counsel, The Money Services Roundtable. Hearing before the Subcommittee on Financial Institutions and Consumer Credit of the Committee on Financial Services, U.S. House of Representatives, 112th Congress, Second Session, Serial No. 112-139, 9 (June 21, 2012). *See also,* Timothy P. Daly, Senior Vice President, Global Public Policy, The Western Union Company. Id. at 49. ("Recent developments in money transmitter regulation have been positive for both consumers and regulated entities, as examinations of multi-state organizations have grown more efficient, effective and consistent.").

[14] The Enhanced CSBS/MTRA Nationwide Cooperative Agreement for MSB Supervision, *available at* http://www.csbs.org/regulatory/Cooperative-Agreements/Documents/MSB/MSBCooperativeAgreement010512clean.pdf.

[15] Braz Transfers Cease and Desist Order, *available at* http://www.mass.gov/ocabr/business/banking-services/banking-legal-resources/enforcement-actions/2013-dobenforcement-actions/braz04012013.html.

[16] Braz Transfers was licensed in 7 of the 14 states currently using NMLS to license MSBs. According to NMLS Consumer Access, the company is no longer authorized to do business in any of these states. *See* http://www.nmlsconsumeraccess.org/Entity Details.aspx /COMPANY/907744.

[17] Memorandum of Understanding between the Internal Revenue Service and the States concerning Money Services Businesses and Certain Other Non-bank Financial Institutions. *Available at* http://www.csbs.org/regulatory/Cooperative-Agreements/Documents/IRS-StatesBSA MOU 4-22-2005.pdf.

[18] "The Bureau shall coordinate with . . . State regulators, as appropriate, to promote consistent regulatory treatment of consumer financial and investment products and services." Dodd-Frank Act § 1015, *codified at* 12 U.S.C. 5495.

[19] Memorandum of Understanding Between the Consumer Financial Protection Bureau, the Conference of State Bank Supervisors, and the Other Signatories Hereto On the Sharing of Information for Consumer Protection and Other Purposes. *Available at* http://www.csbs.org/regulatory/Cooperative-Agreements/Documents/CFPB%20CSBS%20MOU.pdf.

[20] The six state regulatory associations are the American Association of Residential Mortgage Regulators, Conference of State Bank Supervisors, Money Transmitter Regulators Association, National Association of Consumer Credit Administrators, North American Collection Agency Regulatory Association, and National Association of Credit Union Supervisors.

[21] 2013 CFPB-State Supervisory Coordination Framework. *Available at* http://www.csbs.org /regulatory/Cooperative-Agreements/Documents/2013-CFPB.pdf.

[22] The SCC is comprised of representatives of the six State Regulatory Associations and is responsible for representing the state system as a single body to the CFPB.

[23] P.L. 110-289. *Codified at* 12 U.S.C. 5101 et seq.

[24] Timothy P. Daly, Senior Vice President, Global Public Policy, The Western Union Company. Hearing before the Subcommittee on Financial Institutions and Consumer Credit of the Committee on Financial Services, U.S. House of Representatives, 112th Congress, Second Session, Serial No. 112-139, 49-50 (June 21, 2012).

[25] Section 1022(c) of the Dodd-Frank Act directs the CFPB to "consult with State agencies regarding requirements or systems (including coordinated or combined systems for registration), where appropriate."

[26] NMLS complies with the moderate baseline security controls contained in National Institute of Standards and Technology (NIST) Special Publication 800-53, and is fully accredited (FISMA Certification and Accreditation) by the Consumer Financial Protection Bureau. Technical Details and Data Security Protocols for NMLS are available at http://mortgage.nationwidelicensingsystem.org/about/Documents/NMLS%20Data%20Security%20Overview.pdf.

[27] Whether virtual currency is "money" is a critical question. Congress has the sole power to "coin money" and "regulate the value thereof" under Article I, Section 8 of the Constitution. Conversely, Article I, Section 10 prohibits states from coining money and from "mak[ing] any Thing but gold and silver Coin a Tender in Payment of Debts." If virtual currency is not money, the states must determine whether it holds monetary value for the purposes of money transmission laws, or whether it is an instrument securing an interest in another currency.

[28] The Electronic Funds Transfer Act requires disclosure and other consumer protections for the transfer of funds.

As technology accelerates payment clearing, disclosures and liability standards will be of the utmost importance. For example, if a virtual currency wallet is hacked, who is responsible for the lost funds?

[29] Article 4A of the Uniform Commercial Code currently governs commercial fund transfers. Though "funds transfer" is broadly defined under the law, the process is reliant on relationships through the banking system.

INDEX

D

G

H

I

J

K

L

M

N

R

S

T

U

V

W

Y

Z